THIS IS NOT MY MEMOIR

THIS IS NOT MY MEMOIR

André Gregory

and

Todd London

FARRAR, STRAUS AND GIROUX
New York

Farrar, Straus and Giroux
120 Broadway, New York 10271

Printed in the United States of America
First edition, 2020

Photographs by Richard Avedon © The Richard Avedon Foundation.

Library of Congress Cataloging-in-Publication Data
Names: Gregory, André, author. | London, Todd, author.
Title: This is not my memoir / André Gregory and Todd London.
Description: First edition. | New York : Farrar, Straus and Giroux, 2020.
Identifiers: LCCN 2019056431 | ISBN 9780374298548 (hardcover)
Subjects: LCSH: Gregory, André. | Theatrical producers and directors—
    United States—Biography. | Actors—United States—Biography.
Classification: LCC PN2287.G678 A3 2020 | DDC 792.02/33092 [B]—dc23
LC record available at https://lccn.loc.gov/2019056431

Designed by Richard Oriolo

Our books may be purchased in bulk for promotional, educational, or
business use. Please contact your local bookseller or the Macmillan
Corporate and Premium Sales Department at 1-800-221-7945,
extension 5442, or by e-mail at MacmillanSpecialMarkets@macmillan.com.

www.fsgbooks.com
www.twitter.com/fsgbooks • www.facebook.com/fsgbooks

1   3   5   7   9   10   8   6   4   2

For Cindy
Till the end of time.
—A.G.

For Karen
—T.L.

*One must wait until the evening to see
how splendid the day has been.*

—SOPHOCLES

THIS IS NOT MY MEMOIR

1

WHEN I WAS A FRESHMAN at Harvard in 1952, I had horrible roommates and got slightly depressed. As a consequence, I moved into an awful run-down hotel in Boston to avoid them. When I went for walks at night, I would pass the Old Howard, Boston's oldest and most famous burlesque house. I kept returning night after night, because of a stripper called Princess Totem Pole. I called her the Antonin Artaud of striptease, after the mad French artist who envisioned the "theater of cruelty."

The Princess had built herself a raked stage, on which were great green abstract leaves she had painted. Upstage there was a large totem pole, with red lights that blinked on and off like eyes. She gyrated and bumped to the music of Yma Sumac, a Jewish

American girl from Long Island who passed herself off as a Peruvian princess. Two large blackbirds would strip Princess Totem Pole. They would peck at her clothes, and the clothes would fall to the ground. Eventually, I became the Princess's assistant. One of my jobs was to feed the blackbirds.

After telling people this story for years, I decided that it was so unbelievable, so outrageous, that it could not possibly have happened. I must have made it up. So I stopped telling it.

MY YOUNGEST BROTHER, Peter, says there are three stages in a life: Youth, Middle Age, and You're-looking-great! I've reached the age of You're-looking-great, and it's all a mystery. Gloria Steinem cites a Native American saying that old age is, like childhood, a time of wonder, because both are near to the unknown.

And what a wonder my life has been. Or at least it has been a wonder to me. So many stories. I can hardly believe it all happened. As the narrator of my favorite childhood radio show would say each week, "incredible but true." How true? Who can say for sure? Stories are slippery creatures, a bit like dreams, composed of what actually happened, filtered over time through the prism of selective memory.

GIVEN THE AMOUNT OF TIME I generally rehearse the plays I direct—sometimes four years, sometimes as many as fourteen— my next play, Ibsen's *Hedda Gabler*, could be ready for an audience in time for my 100th birthday (as of this writing I am eighty-five years old). Yesterday as we were walking through a graveyard, my wife, Cindy, made me promise to live another twenty years. If I don't, she said, she'll kill me. And does it really matter if I complete the play? Isn't the joy of work in the doing? Isn't it the process itself that matters?

MANY YEARS AFTER I allegedly worked for Princess Totem Pole, I ran into a college classmate as I was leaving a restaurant. He greeted me warmly, as if we were old friends. Then he said: "God, remember how I used to come visit you at the Old Howard when you worked with that stripper? What was her name—Princess something-or-other—with those great big blackbirds?"

So it was true all along.

WE PERFORM THREE CRUCIAL ACTIONS in our lives. One is meeting the partner with whom we will spend our years, if we are lucky enough to do so. One is choosing a vocation— or surrendering to the vocation that chooses us. And the last is finding a spiritual teacher, should we be blessed to find one.

Our vocations come to us very early in life. My friend Richard Avedon, the photographer, once said that as a relatively small child, he would put up a black curtain in his doorway, poke a hole through it, and spend the day watching his family through his improvised lens. The birth of a photographer. Luis Miguel Dominguín, one of the great bullfighters of all time, was already, at the age of two, carving little bulls out of wood. The birth of a bullfighter. By the time my family arrived in America I had experienced so much—violence, dictatorship (including within my family), war, and flight. I already had so many stories to tell. That was my initiation into the world of the artist. You don't necessarily celebrate or appreciate your vocation. In fact, at times, you wish you could escape it. But it never leaves you alone.

I WAS BORN IN PARIS IN 1934 to Russian Jewish parents who had fled to France after years in Germany. Hitler was elected Führer three months after I was born. Two years later the Spanish Civil War and the Moscow Show Trials began. More than eighty years have passed, and I still don't know exactly what my parents did to survive, what kind of deals my father had to make to get away from both Stalin and Hitler.

While our life in Paris was beyond comfortable, the disquieting truth of what it meant to be Jewish in Europe at that time was coming into focus. My parents' friends were leaving without saying goodbye; the choice to depart couldn't have been easy. And to where? America? To my cosmopolitan parents, Grisha Josefowitz and Lydia Sliosberg, America seemed dangerous, disturbing, devoid of culture. America for them was John Dillinger gunned down in front of a movie theater, the gangster Al Capone, and the kidnapping of the Lindbergh child. They weren't ready to leave their apartment in Paris, the city they loved, the world they loved. The only thing that could persuade them to flee to the United States was an even greater fear: the fear of Adolf Hitler and the coming of a second world war.

MY PARENTS MET in the late twenties shortly after Stalin came to power. My father, who had worked with Leon Trotsky during the USSR's New Economic Policy, exporting furs to the United States, was by this time a representative in Moscow for IG Farben, a huge German chemical conglomerate, which a decade later would develop Zyklon B, the gas used in the Nazi death camps. Working for IG Farben meant my father had a German passport as well as a Russian one.

The Soviet secret police wanted one of its own traveling back and forth between Germany and the Soviet Union. As a Soviet representative with IG Farben, he was perfect, except for one thing: He wasn't a member of the Communist Party. They needed their go-between to be a member of the Party. And so they arrested him. His arrest, he theorized, was a first attempt to get him to join. Once released, though, he used his German passport to escape to Berlin. He would spend the next several years trying to get my mother out of Moscow, too. (They had not yet married and, though they hardly knew each other, he had decided she was the one.)

Even before he left Russia for Berlin, my father worked to help other family members leave. He spent time in Warsaw, meeting with the Soviets, who had a small office there in which you could negotiate—as you would with Turkish rug merchants—for relatives already trapped in the Soviet Union. You would offer $10,000 for visas; the Soviets would demand $20,000. Somehow, by the time the war began in 1939, my father had succeeded in getting out of the USSR every single relative that he and my mother had there.

AFTER MY FATHER FLED THE USSR, he made a fortune in Weimar Berlin, one of the wildest cities in all of Europe at the time. The city of Marlene Dietrich and Louise Brooks, and, within a few years, groundbreaking films like *Nosferatu* and *The Cabinet of Dr. Caligari.* Dada and the new German Expressionism had taken root. All kinds of excitement awaited him: brothels for men and for women, nudity, nightclubs, freedom. He made money fast and drove a fancy sports car. Even as he worked to reunite with my mother, who was stuck in Russia, he had a girlfriend who was a dancer at the Berlin Opera.

While my father's life was a cabaret, my dear, Mother was fighting the realities of everyday life in a dictatorship. When her wealthy father was sent to prison, the Communists seized their spacious home. They moved my mother and grandmother into an overcrowded former Leningrad brothel. The lice there were so prolific that the women shaved their heads. They set the legs of the bed they shared in buckets of gasoline to prevent the lice from climbing onto the mattress. One day at the window of the brothel, the story goes, someone began to shout. Everyone ran to look. The rats of Leningrad, starving, abandoning their empty granaries, were marching in a long line to drown themselves in the river.

Four years slipped by. My mother could hardly remember the man she was to marry. But suddenly, out of nowhere, he found a way to save her. He paid an impoverished German man with easy passage in and out of the USSR to "marry" her and bring her to Berlin. By the time my mother reached Germany, though, she and my father had all but forgotten each other. My father had become a sophisticate, and my destitute mother, a refugee from the Soviet Union, had never seen a lobster and didn't know how to peel a banana. They didn't even like each other. So why did they get married? I'll never know.

BEFORE WE EVENTUALLY settled in the United States, my father kept us on the run, all the while laying the foundations for our future lives. From Berlin he and my mother fled to Paris, where I was born. From there he traveled to London, where my mother, my brother Alexis (born in 1936), and I joined him. We left France just as the Germans prepared to invade Poland in September 1939. The Paris railroad station was a madhouse, as if every Parisian was trying to get somewhere else. Our mother, in a station mobbed with people fleeing, asked a blind man to help us with our luggage. He did.

We arrived at our London hotel. I saw my father standing on the grand staircase and burst into hysterical sobbing. I couldn't stop. My parents were great survivors, but they were wretched parents, negligent and self-absorbed, petty and often mean. My father, who'd gone so far to escape tyrants, was a bit of a tyrant himself. So why did I cry so hard when I saw him waiting for us in London? Had I missed him so much, or had I hoped never to see him again? Or was it simply the relief of feeling "safe" after the bedlam of getting out of France?

We spent about six months in London preparing for war. Alexis and I, like most children, were fitted for gas masks. Finally, my father, the escape artist, got us a rare booking on a ship bound for Canada. I was five years old.

Our sister ship sailed at the same time, maybe a mile away. One afternoon it was torpedoed. I can still see the scene in my head: survivors struggling in the Atlantic, rescued passengers sleeping in the hallways. I can still feel the mixture of excitement and terror when the ship's alarm shrieked suddenly and we ran for the lifeboats. The alarm sounded many times, and each time we would run to the boats. They would lower us partway over the side of the ship, and we would hang there. When would we, too, be torpedoed?

. . .

BY THE TIME I was of school age, we were in New York City.

I attended St. Bernard's, a private school in a little British enclave on the Upper East Side, established to train repressed, polite, withdrawn little WASPs, who would in later years head great institutions: banks, law firms, and charitable foundations.

We had three teachers: the headmaster, Mr. Jenkins, a pompous, balding, overweight Colonel Blimp, straight out of Dickens; Captain Fry, a handsome World War I hero; and the hunchbacked Mr. Strange (I'm not kidding), also out of Dickens, who would often sit at his desk leering at us as he cleaned his long, dirty nails with a lead pencil.

The first day of school my mother and my nanny, Isee, had to drag me screaming into the place. I was terrified. It took the school nurse over an hour to calm me down and lead me, petrified, to my classroom.

I was one of only three Jews at St. Bernard's, including my brother Alexis and an Italian boy whose Jewish father had bankrolled Mussolini. Hardly kosher. There was no way at that time that parents could get two Jewish sons into a school like this without telling a whopping fib. Our name had been changed from Josefowitz to Gregory. The family fib was that we were not Jews but aristocratic White Russians who had survived the Bolshevik Revolution. The school bought it. Or maybe that year they were short on tuition. In truth, they probably knew we were Jews, but I didn't. In those days, I actually believed we were Russian aristocrats.

But we weren't. Anti-Semitism, as I would soon learn, had followed us all to America.

· · ·

IT WAS THERE, at St. Bernard's, where I found my calling. It began with an ill-fated crush on a girl. Her name was Patsy Cavendish. It was my second-to-last year at St. Bernard's, and our innocent puppy love played out in letters and poems. I wrote her poems, and she wrote back, which is how we carried on into the summer until one day, unexpectedly, the letters stopped. So I wrote her some more and sent them off. Nothing. I was heartbroken. After a week or two I forgot all about it.

Later, as the fall semester was upon us, two friends and I were returning from Central Park when Patsy appeared on the balcony of her family's new apartment. Surprisingly, she invited us up to listen to music and drink Cokes. Sometime after, her father appeared and dragged me from the room and threw me forcefully down the back stairs. At school the next day I was summoned to the headmaster's office. I was grilled for a long time, forced to admit what "I had done." But since I knew nothing about sex, I had no idea what they were talking about. To make matters worse, the headmaster made an example of me later in front of the entire student body. The fact that I was one of the most accomplished students in my class made no difference. It was humiliating.

The school officials told Phillips Exeter Academy, where I had been accepted for ninth grade, that I was morally unfit and revoked their recommendation. I cried uncontrollably.

Home, at the time, was no more hospitable. My father was slipping into depression, a darkness that would come to impact our little family. My mother had no time to deal with my school problems. She accepted the school's version of the events without question and insisted that I make things right by apologizing, which I did, knowing within myself that I had done nothing wrong. It's a terrible thing to be punished for telling the truth. It would take me years to forgive my mother.

Nonetheless, the episode turned me into a pariah at school, humiliated and lonely in a way I would never feel again. Other students treated me poorly. If I danced with a girl at a party, another boy would immediately cut in. The school, too, downplayed or ignored my accomplishments. I won a prize for an essay, "Woodrow Wilson, Hero of a Lost Cause." At the awards ceremony, however, they announced that no prize would be given that year.

The one thing they could *not* take away was my role as Petruchio in *The Taming of the Shrew*. I had studied the part all summer, and it was too close to opening night for anyone else to come in and steal my spot. I must admit that before I took the stage, I was a very polite boy who never openly showed hostility toward others. But as I looked at the audience of well-heeled gentiles, the very people who had shamed me and turned me into an outcast, I channeled a rage through Shakespeare's dialogue I had never expressed before. Suddenly, in that moment, I learned the therapeutic power of acting.

From that moment on I could not live without the theater. It was my drug to relieve the pain of living. I had found my calling. And so, out of this petty but to me real and awful injustice—one of the prime traumas of my childhood—my vocation seized me.

3

F OR EUROPEAN ÉMIGRÉS WHO FLED the Nazi Holocaust, Southern California became the American Riviera. There were few automobiles, because gas was rationed. There had been little new building. Instead of being filled with high-rises as it is today, Westwood was a simple college town with one little cinema, one collegiate clothing store, and a bookstore. Shopping in Westwood, you could leave your children to wander barefoot and alone in the quiet streets. It was a paradise of lemon groves, orange groves, avocado farms, and, everywhere, flowers flowers flowers.

From about 1941 to 1948 we spent summers in a beautiful house on Sunset Boulevard, rented to us by Thomas Mann, who had written *Joseph in Egypt* there. The house had a stone bridge over the swimming pool, covered with mosaic and tile, like something out of Hearst's San Simeon. My parents were young; they were making money. My father was buying up real estate—including the Brentwood Country Club—at depressed, prewar prices. Later, when he succumbed to bipolar disorder, he would lose his nerve and liquidate too early, missing out on millions of dollars of profit. With 129 acres in central Los Angeles, the club he sold his share of is now worth billions, I believe.

There were parties all the time, and my parents' parties were filled with movie stars. I don't know how they met them. According to my mother's best friend, you could pay a woman in Hollywood to introduce you to celebrities. As my parents told it, though, in pre-Hitler Berlin, statesmen, businessmen, painters, and actors all socialized together. They had become friendly with Marlene Dietrich there, and it was she who, during our summers in Hollywood, introduced them to all these celebrities. However it happened, the house was filled with the likes of Abbott and Costello, Walter Pidgeon, Greer Garson, Charles Boyer, George Burns and Gracie Allen, the Marx Brothers, Erich von Stroheim, Greta Garbo, and Fred Astaire. These parties raged on as the war raged overseas.

When it came to work, mother was lazy, but she came alive in the evenings, like a vampire. She loved going to parties and loved throwing them.

She certainly had *something*. Brilliant artists, celebrities, and, especially, classical musicians adored her. Some of the great musicians of her time—Toscanini and Heifetz—sought her company. What did they see in her? When Vladimir Horowitz was having a nervous breakdown, we would go to his small Hollywood home, and he and Mother would play gin rummy before dinner. Horowitz was still recording during his crisis, but was unable to perform.

Yet, after these dinners, he would sit down at the piano and play just for us.

My mother was witty, stylish, and sarcastic, but for all the romance around her, she was, to me, unknowable. She could certainly be seductive. One night I caught her in the garden kissing Errol Flynn behind a bush. She was having an affair.

THIS PARADE OF STARS and the comic drama of their comings and goings certainly influenced my love of the theater. But something else from our Hollywood life may have impacted me even more profoundly: the radio.

My parents' friend Basil Rathbone had originated and, for years, played the role of Sherlock Holmes in the movies. Rathbone had a weekly radio show, *The Sherlock Holmes Hour*, and he invited my brother Alexis and me to some of the taping sessions. I was fascinated—obsessed really—by the tricks of the sound technician, the way some gizmo could create the illusion of horse hooves on cobblestone streets, the way two sticks knocked together became sinister footsteps in a sinister corridor, how a foghorn conjured up all of nineteenth-century London. No need for sets, costumes, or lights. With only sound and words—*emphasis on "words"*—one could create images in the mind of an audience. With nothing but sheer storytelling, the audience could actually *see*.

I loved listening to those radio plays. I would hide the radio under the blankets after bedtime and disappear into my imagination. I remember wanting to listen to my favorite show, *Red Ryder*, but my parents were hogging the radio for news of the D-day invasion of Normandy Beach. They listened all day and into the night, until I missed my other favorite radio program, *Mary Noble, Backstage Wife.*

I WAS GETTING A LESSON from Harvey Snodgrass, tennis pro at the Beverly Hills Hotel, when he suddenly threw his tennis racket up in the air and whooped with joy. Our horrific bomb had just been needlessly dropped on Hiroshima.

We didn't know, and many still don't accept, that we had already won the war, that 94 percent of Japan's cities had been fire-bombed, that we dropped the bomb to impress the Soviets and to justify the vast sums of money we'd spent on this monstrosity. But to my tennis teacher the bomb meant his son would no longer have to fight in this terrible, protracted war. My lesson was canceled, and I went home to find my mother by the radio, sobbing over the bombing. It was the first and last time I ever saw her cry.

ONE OF THE FEW TRIUMPHS of my childhood came, rather perversely, from my mother's affair with Errol Flynn. After one of these romantic, California dreamin' summers, I returned to the awful St. Bernard's School and started boasting to the boys about all the famous people that I knew. They didn't believe me. (Not that I can blame them.) When I wouldn't retract the stories, they beat me up.

My mother got the brilliant idea to invite her lover Errol Flynn, who was in New York, to have lunch at home with us. I would bring a classmate to that lunch, and he would see Flynn in the flesh, get an autograph, and tell everyone at school that I did, in fact, know the famous leading man. Maybe mother did this out of the goodness of her heart, or maybe she did it because I'd threatened to tell my father about them kissing in the bushes if she wasn't nicer to me. (I must have been a nastier child than I remember.) Whatever her reason, the plan was hatched.

Lunch was set for a Sunday at one. By two thirty still no Flynn, and it looked like my reputation would be sunk for good.

My mother called the Waldorf Astoria, where Flynn was staying, but he didn't answer. She leapt into a taxi. When the man at the Waldorf desk wouldn't let her up to the room, she created a scene. She said she was pregnant with Flynn's child (might this have been true?) and that, unless they let her see him, she would talk to the press about it all. She would drag the hotel through the mud. They showed her up.

She found Flynn unconscious in bed next to a woman she assumed was a hooker. She pulled him out of bed, dragged him into a cold shower, dried him off, put him into a cab, and took him to our place, where he had a stiff drink, signed my friend's autograph book, and saved my reputation. My mother had allowed me to become a pariah at St. Bernard's once; this time she gave me a great gift. I not only saved face, but I became a school celebrity.

4

THERE WAS ANOTHER WOMAN IN MY LIFE, my nanny, Isee, who was more of a mother to my siblings and me than our actual mother.

Isee's story starts in Paris. My mother, walking down the boulevard, bumps into an old friend. Mother complains that she and my father can't take a holiday, because there's no one to take care of her little boy, her two-year-old. The friend introduces Mother to Hilda Copnall, who I would later and ever after call Isee. Isee must've been about nineteen or twenty; she was on her holiday and planning to go back to England to study nursing. She said, "Oh, I could take the boy for a week."

A month later my parents still had not returned. Isee received an envelope with cash inside to take care of their little boy. These envelopes came each week. When they finally returned and discovered that Isee, being so young, had never seen the great capitals of Europe, they gave her more cash and sent her on a nice trip around Europe with me—their little boy—in tow.

Isee had never thought of being a nanny, but when my brother Alexis was born, around the time of our tour of the capitals, she stayed on to take care of the newborn and me. Perhaps she felt sorry for us, so sorry that she was still with us forty-five years later, at Alexis's apartment every day, keeping him company at breakfast, fixing him fine English tea, even making his bed, unable to escape the magnetic pull of our family.

We never knew what I was trying to say when I called her Isee. Was I trying to say, "Oh yes, I see. From now on I'm going to have a nanny instead of a mother?" Or was I calling her "Icy," because she was English and reserved?

She wasn't emotional or demonstrative, didn't hug or kiss us. In fact, I wasn't hugged or kissed until I was an adult. Isee was, though, comforting. It's too long ago to remember all she did for us, but she was there when I woke in the morning, with breakfast on the table. She was there at dinner and when I went to sleep. She was always, always there.

By contrast my parents were absent, even when they were physically there. Early on, they were away preparing for our exit from Europe, laying the groundwork for our survival, for the journey out of the terrifying, disintegrating old world and into a new world, a new life. Later, they were off being socialites, giving parties, going to parties. Their generation believed that children should be seen and not heard. Is this why my parents neither saw nor heard us? Clearly, they had no idea what to do with us.

When I was a baby, before Isee stumbled into our midst, my

high-flying parents discovered I liked the salty taste of caviar. So that's what they fed me, almost exclusively. Finally, sick with malnutrition, I had to be taken to the American Hospital. Around the same time they hired a German governess who, hating the sound of children crying, put Seconal powder into my milk at night. I slept for more than eighteen hours before my mother thought to take me, once again, to the American Hospital, where they pumped my stomach. Instead of being horrified, my parents made the episode a family joke: how for a year after the Seconal poisoning, though I had already learned to walk, I would take a few steps, drop to my knees, and fall into a deep sleep.

My mother also joked about standing on the steps of a European hotel and admiring a baby in a carriage. She said to the governess, "What a beautiful baby." The governess replied, "But Madame, it's yours." She had no talent for mothering, and found this lack in herself funny.

I'm afraid to think what would have happened had Isee not been there to watch over us. Alexis and I took a trial voyage to America on the luxurious S.S. *Normandie* with just our parents. This trip would decide whether or not America was "civilized" enough for our family. When they left us alone in the New York hotel—I was five and he was three—I invented a great game. It was called Ship's Crossing. Alexis would be the passenger and I the ship's captain. Payment for an Atlantic crossing was a lock of Alexis's hair, which I gleefully extracted with a large pair of scissors. We made many crossings before our parents returned to the hotel to see his head covered with only a few, rough patches of his blond, formerly curly hair.

How do I remember all this at such a distance of years? I don't, except for bits and pieces. Then how do I know these things? I know all this because my parents told me. Over and over. Their stories have become my memories. How could they tell such incriminating things about themselves?

I HAVE SUCH SWEET, full memories of being sent to stay with Isee's parents and two strapping brothers in the industrial north of England. Her brothers would walk with me along the many quiet canals that wound through the countryside. They taught me how to fish. I was fed shepherd's pie and large roasts with mashed potatoes and gravy. They fattened me up, which may have been the purpose of the trip. Isee's mother was heavy and warm. They fussed over me. One day I woke from my daily nap and saw a web with a large spider in the middle. I broke into hysterics. The entire family rushed to my bedside. They cradled me. They cared.

I returned with a heavy heart from Isee's family home to the loneliness of Paris, which might explain why I hate Paris to this day. It was a sad train trip back.

Isee was beside us when we finally crossed the ocean to move from Europe to the New World. It seemed natural that she would leave her own family to journey with ours. She was in New York through my school years, and right up until my marriage. When my youngest brother, Peter, was born, seven years after Alexis, she took care of him, too. (Alexis and I, wanting a sister, had walked into the maternity ward, hoping to trade Peter in for a girl.) She would sit on the bench in Central Park with the other English nannies, knitting, gossiping, and keeping an eye on us. Alexis and I would climb the rocks and hide in the bushes, playing English Fight Nazis. With the prerogative of a big brother, I always made Alexis the Nazi.

Each Sunday, Isee would bake us delicious, authentically English shepherd's pie. On Fridays she would take Alexis and me to the movies, either the 72nd Street Loews or the 86th Street RKO, each one a grand, ornate movie palace. The RKO had a vaulted ceiling of dark velvety blue, twinkling with thousands of tiny stars. Temple columns rose up. Monumental statues of the Pharaohs stood guard, painted with faux gold. An ancient Egyptian hodgepodge. Few such palaces exist now, Radio City Music Hall being one of the last.

In those ancient times—mine, not Egypt's—a day at the movies included a feature, a second B movie, previews of coming attractions, a newsreel, a cartoon, and a short. After this sumptuous feast Alexis, Isee, and I would journey on to a nearby luncheonette for ice cream sodas.

Peter, nine years younger than me, was a toddler when Isee met Stanley, a tall, rather handsome Englishman living in America. Stanley's father had been an inspector in Scotland Yard's Jack the Ripper case, and a bit of Jack the Ripper may have brushed off on him, because he was a small-time sadist, regularly pinching both Alexis and me quite hard. He moved in, and they had a son.

On the day they were married, in a pretty Episcopal church on Wall Street, Alexis, Peter, and I pressed close against her bridal gown as she prepared to enter the church. People passing must have been touched by the scene. They surely assumed that Isee was a war widow, remarrying, with her three father-orphaned children clinging to her skirts.

Isee and Stanley went to England for their honeymoon, and my mother took Alexis, Peter, and me to the south of France. We'd never been alone with her. We freaked out. No Isee!! Who was this nervous, uncomfortable woman calling herself our mother?

Without Isee total chaos broke out. Alexis began to sleepwalk. Peter developed hysterical paralysis from the waist down. A specialist came from Paris to diagnose him. I spent long, rainy days playing gin rummy for money with my mother, winning and, so, driving her nuts. My parents contacted Isee in England, and she cut her honeymoon short and returned to make our family whole again.

Over the years Isee became obsessed with the life of our family—where we went, who we knew, details of my parents' celebrity parties and voyages, who said what, and so on. She became the source of much of what I know about my parents' lives. This must have been hard on her and Stanley's son. Our world became her life, maybe even more than the lives of her own husband and child.

I CAN'T TELL YOU who Isee really was, because, to my great regret, I kept my distance from her. I didn't want a nanny. I wanted a "real" mother, and I couldn't accept that she was exactly that: my only mother. My brothers and I have often said that Isee kept the three of us out of the loony bin.

I visited her little apartment in the East 60s decades later, after Stanley died. We were standing in the lobby doorway when a torrential rain began. Isee and I stood close together, waiting for the downpour to stop. She looked into my eyes, her own filled with love and caring, and said: "You look tired. Are you all right?"

I will never forget that moment. I was so stunted in the art of loving that I couldn't reciprocate her tenderness, couldn't touch her face or take her in my arms. I couldn't forgive her for reminding me of all the ways my "real" mother wasn't my real mother at all.

When Isee was dying, I visited her in the hospital only once. It was a brief, polite courtesy call, not that of a son visiting his dying mother. In time I would often visit dying friends. I would learn to be helpful, tender, and loving, but too late for Isee.

5

I DIDN'T LIKE HARVARD. The ancient teachers (probably only in their thirties or forties) never talked to you. They read lectures at you, the same lectures they gave year after year after year. I liked mingling with the women at Radcliffe, though, and I found my first real love there: Ina.

I loved her, but given my childhood, I couldn't imagine anyone loving me. I never even held her hand, though we were together all the time. One evening, walking together in an old Cambridge graveyard—it was a full moon—she decided to just go for it. She kissed me passionately. It was too much for me. I fainted.

Another night, after we'd dated for about five months, I went to pick Ina up at her dorm. She was gone. Disappeared. No forwarding address.

It was years before I found out what had happened. She had fallen in love with me, too, but couldn't bring herself to tell me that she was engaged. Her fiancé was a marine captain, serving in the Korean War. His name was Maco. He came from Waco, Texas. (Yes, Maco from Waco.) Ina had gone missing to tell her parents she couldn't marry Maco. She wanted to marry me. Her father said, "Speak to your mother." Her mother said, "We have hired the orchestra, we have hired the caterer, all girls go through this." And so she did.

The period following university was both empty and full, full of rejection. I graduated from Harvard in 1956 and dreamed of starting at Yale Drama School the following fall. I scheduled an interview with a legendary dean there. His words have never left me: "You know, it's so hard to tell anything from a young face. Tabula rasa, a young face. But occasionally, just occasionally, I do meet a young person who so clearly has no talent whatsoever. I have to beg you, don't do it. The theater is impossible enough if you do have talent, but if you don't . . . Become a lawyer [was my father speaking through him?] or a doctor."

So I joined the army.

I WAS ASSIGNED to an experimental program in which marines trained regular soldiers. We took forty-mile marches through sand with forty-five-pound backpacks strapped on. We crawled on our bellies at night with real bullets whizzing overhead; one young man panicked, stood up, and was killed. We did God-knows-how-many chin-ups to get into breakfast. We learned to take big breaths, enter huts filled with tear gas, and, while blind-folded, dismantle our rifles and put them back together before taking another breath. We ran across fields holding bayonets and screaming, "KILL KILL." I was good at all of it. On breaks, aspiring gentile that I was, I would memorize psalms.

After this army/marine training, I felt strong and coordinated. My golf game had improved, and I had developed a discipline that would stay with me through sixty-five years of directing. Even in my eighties, I do sixty push-ups every day.

MY FATHER WAS AN AVID POKER PLAYER, and one night he lost a lot of money to Jean Dalrymple, the Broadway producer. At the request of the State Department, Dalrymple was about to travel to Brussels to supervise all the American entertainment for the first World's Fair since the war. "I've lost so much money to you tonight," my father said to her. "Why don't you give my son a job?" (Before that, he'd gotten me, through a friend, a job as assistant director on a Maidenform bra commercial.) If I had to work in the theater—a prospect he claimed would give him a heart attack—at least he'd make sure I earned some money.

And so I became an assistant stage manager at the American Pavilion of the Brussels Expo 58. The American Pavilion was like a cruise ship that never dropped anchor. Young people went there to work and wound up falling in love and getting married. I was one of them.

Mercedes Nebelthau worked as a guide there. She was the most astoundingly beautiful woman I have ever seen, with a re-semblance to Ingrid Bergman, but even more striking. Chiquita, as she was always known, had been born in Bremen to a German father and Argentine mother. In other words, she wasn't an American. She spoke six languages fluently, though, and so had landed a job at the pavilion.

Chiquita grew up in Bremen, the daughter of a father who believed, probably rightly, that she was illegitimate, and a mother who married five times. According to Chiquita's best friend, Gus, Chiquita's mother was returning to Germany on a passenger ship from her native Argentina when she had an affair with an Argentine man, possibly Jewish, which resulted in the birth of her daughter.

Chiquita's father was cold, withdrawn, and distant. He was the kind of tyrant who, if the cook brought dinner late, would empty the soup tureen on the floor. He was in the tobacco business. When World War II broke out, he transformed his tobacco factory into one that made treads for the tanks the German army would ride into Russia, the tanks that ultimately littered the frozen Russian landscape like dead carcasses. He went through a denazification program after the war. His family claimed this association with the Nazis was a case of mistaken identity.

Chiquita and her mother got out of Nazi Germany under the most unusual circumstances. Her parents were about to divorce, but, in a clumsy attempt to patch things up, Chiquita's father gave her mother the gift of a new, bright red Mercedes-Benz convertible. Soon after, the German army, quietly planning to invade Poland, and needing vehicles for their encroachment, took the car away.

Chiquita's father was invited sometime later to a tobacco convention in Hamburg, and he took his flamboyant wife with him. An unexpected guest showed up at the opening night reception: Adolf Hitler. A line formed. Hitler shook hands with the guests, one by one.

When Chiquita's mother got to Hitler, she took his hand, looked him in the eye, smiled, and said, "You know, my husband gave me a new red Mercedes-Benz sports car, and your army has taken it from me. If you continue to steal from beautiful women, there will be no beautiful women left in Germany. And a country without beautiful women is a country without a soul." Two days later a new red Mercedes-Benz sports car was delivered to the house. Chiquita's mother put her daughter in the car—Chiquita was three years old—and the two of them drove to Switzerland and never came back.

WE KNEW EACH OTHER for only a few months before we got married, months filled with lots of passion and many fights. No sex, though. It was the fifties, remember, and we were among the many couples who didn't "do it" before marriage. In the fifties you got married, men and women, to escape being "an old maid" once you turned twenty-five. You got married to get away from your parents, or just for the promise of ongoing sex. Neither of us really knew who the other one was. That wasn't a priority in those days.

We took our vows at a Catholic altar. Her father only agreed to her marrying a Jew, I believe, because he thought she was not his real daughter. He made me sign a paper, agreeing to bring up our children as Catholics. I did so. I am a man of few regrets, but I deeply regret not teaching my kids about Judaism, their own heritage. After my children were grown, I studied with a rabbi who argued that assimilation was the second Holocaust.

At our wedding party, the formally attired guests were arranged around a long table at a Bremen hotel. Young blond men still wearing medals from the war. The reception looked like a Luftwaffe reunion. What the hell was I doing there? We were children—I was twenty-four, Chiquita twenty-three. We hardly knew each other. Just like my parents.

She was ill for most of our honeymoon, which didn't prevent us from having a terrible fight. I had gone to great lengths to get tickets for the London production of *My Fair Lady*, and she hated it. How could anyone hate *My Fair Lady*? How could the two of us be so different? The fight was so bad that we decided to get divorced as soon as we got to America. We would still go to Jamaica, our honeymoon spot, to rest up for the divorce.

The divorce never happened. Instead we settled in New York, a city she hated immediately. The fights began again. Chiquita was volatile and lost in a new land. I was angry, battered from my own awful childhood, lost and afraid I would never have a career in the theater. We never discussed our problems, kept things on the surface.

And so began our marriage, 1950s-style. I looked for a job, and Chiquita spent the days at home in New York, which remained, to her, a friendless, alien, and unlikable city.

6

ERLAND JOSEPHSON, the great Swedish actor, once said to me: "I went to great teachers to learn about the voice. I went to great teachers to learn about the emotions. I went to great teachers to learn about expressing oneself physically. What I would now like to do is find a teacher who could show me how to walk down to the footlights and—by just standing there, by doing nothing—be like a lighthouse illuminating and giving hope to the audience."

Might this be part of the task of being human: to keep working on oneself, to go higher on the ladder so your life can be more like a work of art itself?

. . .

I WAS ALWAYS LOOKING for a teacher. I was always looking for a father.

Gordon Craig was my first great inspiration, and he was long dead. The illegitimate son of Ellen Terry, a legendary English actress of the nineteenth century, Craig, a set designer and director, was a visionary who could not fulfill his visions. He could not make them concrete on the stage. He was one of those marvels of nature who inspired me when I was still a teenager. I couldn't see his work, but I could read his books and, through immersing myself in his drawings and designs, I could dream. I could dream about the possibilities of a theater not rooted in soap opera naturalism. I could imagine a theater that was extraordinary, a theater of marvels.

I loved a story about Craig being invited by Stanislavski to direct *Hamlet* at the Moscow Art Theatre. Craig made the actors extend their arms, as if they were more than human—long, long extensions like figures in a Giacometti sculpture. They put out their arms as far as humans could, but he would run down the aisles, leap onto the stage, pull their arms—or try to—farther out of their shoulders. "Longer! Longer!" he cried, frustrated by the shortness of a human arm.

Many years ago I was on the little ferry going from the island of Lipari to Naples. On deck I began a conversation with a rather elderly, distinguished, well-dressed Italian gentleman. I was wearing a pea jacket, and early in the conversation he asked me where I got the jacket. "New York," I answered. "Yes, but where in New York?" he asked. I told him I purchased it on Canal Street. "Where on Canal Street is the shop where you got your pea jacket?" he asked. "I have always wanted that kind of coat," said the distinguished Italian gentleman.

We talked about other things, about Lipari, about Italy, and so on. But every once in a while he would return to the pea jacket. Finally, as we came into harbor he said, "May I ask you what kind of work you do?" "I'm a theater director," I replied. "Oh," he said. "Perhaps you have heard of my great-great-uncle Gordon Craig?" I took off my jacket and put it on the man's shoulders.

PERHAPS WHAT WE CALL a vocation—a calling—is something passed on from generation to generation. People reaching into the well of time. In the theater this calling stretches back through Jerzy Grotowski to Yevgeny Vakhtangov to Vsevolod Meyerhold to Stanislavski and Eleonora Duse and Gordon Craig to Molière to Shakespeare to Sophocles. They call us. I don't know how they do this, but perhaps they do. This is what my friend the psychologist James Hillman termed *taking our place in the long line of our ancestors.*

BERTOLT BRECHT, the great German director and playwright, was my next inspiration, but he, too, had died before I could know him. A professor of mine at Harvard, Robert Chapman, found out that I was going to work at the Brussels Expo and told me, "You must visit the Brecht theater." And so I did. The World's Fair in Brussels ended and, while Chiquita and I planned our wedding, I made my way to Berlin. I had no idea what "the Brecht theater" was and no inkling that it would change my life. I went for a weekend and stayed nearly two months.

East Berlin under Soviet occupation was terrifying. With little electricity there were no streetlights. The only buildings that were lit at night were embassies, theaters, and the legendary Hotel

Adlon. That was it. You could turn a corner and find yourself facing a Soviet tank. On certain holidays the East German army would march for hours, goose-stepping like Nazis. The place was incredibly poor. There was nothing in the stores. Nowhere to eat. Bookstores carried hardly anything but propaganda books and plays by Brecht. The city seemed shrouded, sad.

Taking the subway through Friedrichstrasse from West to East Berlin was a frightening way to reach a frightening city. I was headed to the famed Berliner Ensemble, considered the greatest theater in Europe, but I was on my own. I have never liked being alone; alone feels *lonely*. This time it also felt strange and scary. I didn't know what was waiting for me. I didn't speak German. The border was swarming with toughs, cold-eyed secret police, recruited from the farthest east of East Germany, where they were unlikely to have friends or relatives in Berlin. They could be ruthlessly impersonal. I was carrying, for comfort, a book. A guard grabbed it and tore it to pieces. I have always loved the theater and been willing to go anywhere to find it, to learn, to be inspired. But this journey through the postwar world, in my early twenties, terrified me.

And then I arrived at the Berliner Ensemble: Mecca.

Brecht and his wife, Helene Weigel, had founded the theater in 1949, when he'd returned to Berlin from his wartime exile in the United States, from which he'd fled after being compelled to testify before the House Un-American Activities Committee. He'd made the company a seminal, groundbreaking world theater, largely through his new productions of his own previously staged plays, including *Mother Courage and Her Children* and *The Caucasian Chalk Circle*, as well as, later, premieres of unproduced plays he'd written during the war, directed by his team of associate directors. After all, they were a Marxist collective. The work was steeped in Marxism and, to some extent, Brecht's own theatrical theories. Plays were rehearsed over long periods of time with extraordinary rigor and painstaking precision. Brecht had died in 1956, two years before I arrived on his doorstep.

The outside of the Ensemble's building, Theater am Schiffbauerdamm, was still pockmarked with bullets from when the Soviets took over Berlin. Even the men's rooms were riddled with bullet holes, a jarring contrast to a theater so full of energy and light. The building's interior was striking, unexpected. Brecht had borrowed or purchased golden baroque angels from all over the Soviet zone, and he'd covered the auditorium, like a wedding cake, with these cherubs and with red plush carpeting. The productions, on the other hand, were often sparse, minimal, and confrontational, contradicting the sumptuous surroundings. The set for *Galileo* was three huge walls and a ceiling of glowing, beaten burnt copper. Because everything was scarce, the East German parliament passed legislation "asking" citizens to loan the theater their old copper pipes. These would be replaced with new copper—or so was the hope—at a later date. The past, with all its beauty and horror, literally surrounded the future; the old lived side by side with the new. Brecht always wanted you to think and think and think.

The contradictions were everywhere. In the audience Soviet Politburo big shots and their wives sat elbow to elbow with the Western intellectuals who poured in from around the world. The word was out. The Berliner Ensemble had become known as the finest, most innovative company since the great Russian theaters of the twenties, the pride of the state.

In New York in the 1940s Brecht had noticed that the walls surrounding construction sites had old doors in them, with peepholes so passersby could watch the building going up. Why shouldn't people be able to watch a production going up? And so, each day, about two hundred of us watched rehearsal. Among these eager spectators, at that same time, was a young Polish director named Jerzy Grotowski. We never met.

The marquee poster for the night I arrived read: *Das Leben von Galilei*. I didn't speak a word of German, and I knew only one Brecht play, *The Threepenny Opera*, so I thought I was about to see something called, *The Good Fisherman of Galilee*. *The Life of Galileo* (the actual title) lasted over four hours. I couldn't make out a word, and yet I understood almost everything. "How is that possible?" you might ask. Here's how: Every moment onstage was fully explored; every gesture told not one story but everything important about that story: where the characters came from, what their economic circumstances were, what the dynamics between them signified. They had rehearsed over a long period of time, so that each *event* (a word I'll talk more about later), every piece of the story rang clear and, somehow, became universal.

Brecht's widow, Helene Weigel, was unbelievably hospitable to me. She found me a small apartment, introduced me to a few of the actors, had me over for tea. I even imagined—or did I actually see it?—that she winked at me and threw her skirt up during a musical review.

Years later I realized, to my enormous regret, that Weigel might have wanted to have an affair with me. But I was only twenty-four and didn't realize that women in their fifties had sex. What an adventure that would've been! What a roller coaster!

MY IDEAL THEATER WOULD BE a theater of miracles, and Brecht knew how to make miracles happen. Back in East Berlin someone told him about a marvelous singer performing in the subway, which was still in ruins from being flooded by the Soviet army. Brecht went to hear this young subway singer and, after the performance, told him that he had a beautiful voice. Brecht told the singer about the theater he hoped to create one day and asked if he, Ekkehard Schall, would like to be part of the company. "Before we start work, though, you must develop your body to supplement your voice." Based on this iffy offer, Schall trained to become a high-wire aerialist in Germany, a commitment that went way beyond mere training. It came from the belief that great performance requires great devotion.

Schall played the title role in Brecht's *Arturo Ui*. Ui is a terrifying cartoon version of Hitler crossed with Richard III and Charlie Chaplin. The play takes place in Al Capone's Chicago. At one moment in the play four or five gangsters approach Ui/Hitler to assassinate him. Terrified, Schall/Ui began to froth at the mouth, some kind of black bile. I kid you not. I saw this performance many, many times. It wasn't a trick. The actor then did a triple backward somersault from a standing position, landed on the back of the couch, standing, with two drawn revolvers, and shot his would-be assassins. Now, that is miraculous.

And then there is the miracle of dedication. Schall prepared by watching hours of documentaries on Hitler for two years. He didn't play at Hitler; he *was* Hitler. At the end of the play he walked toward the audience from upstage, screaming about conquering America and France. The audience literally recoiled in horror. The ruins of the Reichstag were only blocks away.

AS I WAS AT THE BEGINNING of my education as a young director, as well as a nervous, nerdy intellectual, I asked Helene Weigel about the *Verfremdungseffekt*, Brecht's famous "alienation effect" theory. The *"V-effekt"* proposes distancing the audience from emotionally identifying with the characters in order to elicit a conscious, intelligent response to dramatic material. This *thinking* response—as opposed to the usual *feeling* one—actively engages the audience, thus inspiring action. By provoking thought and action, Brecht meant to overthrow the passive emotionalism of theater that aims for what Aristotle called *catharsis*. Weigel laughed and said something like, "Don't pay any attention to Bert's bullshit and theoretical nonsense. Just look at the work. Look at the work, and see what you see."

When you looked at Helene Weigel you could see in her face the lines of great experience. This was a fierce woman who, with Brecht, trekked across the Soviet Union to China, through China, traveling on to Los Angeles, in order to escape the Nazis. This was the woman for whom Brecht had written the role of Mother Courage.

"Look at the work," she ordered. And I did. Mostly I watched them rehearse *Arturo Ui*, but the first rehearsals I attended were for a one-act play, *The Jewish Wife*, that Brecht had written for Weigel in the mid-thirties. I believe they were readying it to reenter the repertory. Brecht had originally directed the play, and Weigel told a story about their work on it that I've never forgotten. In this brief series of three monologues, a Jewish woman married to a successful Aryan doctor prepares to leave Germany and, implicitly, her husband. She calls three close friends to tell them of her plans to emigrate. Each section begins with the line, "I'm leaving."

Each time Weigel said the line, she would begin to weep. "No, no," Brecht barked. "Sentimental! It's sentimental." (This was a dirty word at the Ensemble.) "You only say that because you are a man and don't understand women," Weigel barked back. "I wrote it, damn it, and I know what I wrote," the playwright yelled.

"Well, I have to act it!" replied the actress. They quarreled in front of a large invited audience. "Well, do it again," he commanded.

And she did. More tears. "It's awful. Sentimental." Frustrated, Brecht suggested they rehearse the next day without him. (Rehearsing without the director, in a Marxist collective, meant working with his team of eight associate directors.) The next day, in character, Weigel picked up the phone to call her friends. Brecht was on the other end of the line, having somehow had his phone connected to the one onstage. He started telling her personal stories, jokes about their sex life. This time, when she repeated, "I'm leaving," instead of tears came a chilling laugh. Weigel finished the story by walking to the lip of the stage, and speaking directly to the two hundred observers: "What Bert wanted to teach us is that a woman with the courage to leave everything doesn't cry. She laughs!" Learn, learn, always learning.

I LEARNED MOST OF WHAT I know about directing at the Ensemble: about clarity, about taking the time you need to perfect a work. Theater, I learned from Brecht after his death, is not a casual endeavor. It is Art, no different than painting, musical composition, or novel writing. It is Art and, as such, it deserves the money it needs and the time it needs. And it's worth whatever it takes.

One other thing I learned from my German artistic daddy: Over his desk at the Berliner Ensemble hung a large banner, "SIMPLER AND WITH MORE LAUGHTER."

7

THEATER IS A METAPHOR FOR LIFE: You get kicked onto the stage, you struggle for a few hours with your problems and those of the people playing scenes with you, and then you exit. The curtain falls and, usually, the play is forgotten, just as I will be forgotten.

SOMETIME AFTER RETURNING FROM BERLIN, I got a job as an assistant stage manager at the Phoenix Theatre. A year before, I had been turned away from a sold-out show Off Broadway in the East Village, so I walked up Second Avenue to the Phoenix Theatre at Twelfth Street. The marquee read, *The Chairs* and *The Lesson* by

Eugene Ionesco, titles and a name I didn't know. I got a seat for the preview that night. I was staggered. I had never seen anything like it. The rhythm of the language was unlike any sound I'd heard. I stayed up all night, calling friends to say I'd witnessed a miracle. I needed to work at the Phoenix, and so, having returned from Brussels and Berlin, newly married and soon to be a father, I did.

I worked a benefit performance to raise money for the Phoenix. A lineup of great jazz musicians donated their services to the cause. I was a fresh-faced, polite, Harvard-educated, ignorant young man. I couldn't fathom why it was so hard to get the musicians out of their dressing rooms and onto the stage. I had never even heard of marijuana.

In the run-up to the benefit, there had been trouble concerning one of the lead performers, a singer who wouldn't be allowed to attend. Billie Holiday was in a prison hospital, dying. I had never heard of her, either. Norris Houghton, one of the Phoenix producers, was an old friend of Robert Wagner, New York's mayor. He persuaded the mayor to let Billie Holiday perform one last time. She wanted to perform.

Lady Day arrived at the theater in a prison ambulance. Frail and weak, dying of cirrhosis, she could barely stand at the microphone to sing. I was one of the two stage managers who held her up by the arms, while she sang her very last song. It's been so many years, but in my memory, she sang words like, "I don't care what nobody thinks about me." We helped her back to the ambulance, and she returned to the prison hospital. She died about six weeks later, having never performed again.

WHEN I WAS ABOUT TWELVE I had a spiritual awakening at Radio City Music Hall. We'd had a birthday party in class.

Afterward, all the boys were taken to Radio City to see a movie and the Rockettes. When the Rockettes danced onto the stage with their incredible precision, I thought I was having a vision. For a moment I touched the Divine and was in the presence of what I would later call the Miraculous. I laughed uncontrollably— ecstatic or crazy or both. Not until Brecht's Ensemble would I find a theater with the precision of the Rockettes. And not until Billie Holiday would I encounter a performer willing to risk her life to sing one more song. But that day, years before Berlin and Billie Holiday, I found God—at Radio City Music Hall.

LEE STRASBERG, the guiding patriarch of the Actors Studio and American Method acting, was omnipresent in my world for many years. Twice a week, Tuesday and Friday mornings, dozens of working theater artists and aspirants would attend our church, the Actors Studio, in an actual church on West 44th Street, just up Ninth Avenue from the largest butcher in the city. Unless we had a job, we never missed a service. The High Priest, Lee Strasberg, looked like a Jewish tailor who spent his nights studying Torah.

THERE ARE NO WORDS to describe the excitement and mystery surrounding the Studio. People like Laurence Olivier and the actors of the magnificent Piccolo Teatro di Milano sought an opening to these mysterious sessions, this hallowed actors' church. They came from all over the world. People fought about the validity of what was taught there. Talk shows made fun of what they imagined was taught there. "Method" became a term of worship and of derision. It was such a big part of the zeitgeist that when

Robert (Bobby) Lewis, a fine acting teacher and co-founder of the Studio, gave eight lectures titled "Method or Madness" at the Playhouse Theatre, five thousand people applied to attend.

THE DAY I DIRECTED my first scene for Strasberg was one of the most awful in my life. I had chosen a scene from George Bernard Shaw's *Saint Joan*, in which Joan and her comrades-in-arms wait for battle. A strong wind blows easterly—we see a fluttering pennant stuck in the ground—but they need the wind to turn toward the west to get up the river for a sneak attack. Without this reversal, Joan's army will almost certainly lose. The confident Joan prays to God, who sends voices that only she can hear, for a change in the wind.

Everyone was at the Studio that day—Marilyn Monroe, Paul Newman, Shelley Winters. I presented my scene. Hands went up throughout the audience; everyone wanted to critique the scene. Strasberg, who always sat in the front row, shot his arms into the air to silence them. All other hands went down. He looked at me with his fierce, cold eyes and said, before I had even explained my intentions, "I would like to know if you call that directing. And if you do, I would like to know why."

My eyes were hot with tears. I was mortified. I didn't know what to say. In the silence after his short critique, I left the room. It took me many months to get up the courage to return, months of depression. But I did return. I didn't give up. My calling—that guardian angel born in me—wouldn't allow it.

Strasberg's critique may have been harsh but it was extremely important, and I've remembered it my entire directing life. I had misunderstood the lesson of the Studio. I had thought that emotion was the only goal. My actors were overflowing with feeling and emotion. These feelings and emotions were of little value, Strasberg said, because the director had failed to create what Stanislavski called "the Event." The event of my scene was simple: Military personnel wait for the wind to change. As director, I needed to make it clear that these two characters were at war and that their lives depended on a change in that war—namely a change in the wind. That's the event.

STRASBERG WAS A RABBI of the theater. He had read every single book written on the subject. He could talk for hours, often brilliantly, about the art of the actor. Had it not been for Strasberg and the Actors Studio, we might never have had the generation of great actors who peopled the plays of Tennessee Williams, Arthur Miller, and William Inge, nor the seminal American films from the second half of the twentieth century. I learned a lesson at the Studio that has stayed with me my entire life: The theater, in some fundamental way, belongs to the actor.

STRASBERG WAS AN ARTISTIC FATHER to me, and he was emotionally cut off, just as I was then—shy, withdrawn, and distant. I got permission to visit him at his apartment. I had an important question: If I went into psychoanalysis, could self-knowledge and the lessening of personal pain harm my talent? (I hadn't yet read the work of the legendary Jungian analyst Marie-Louise von Franz. Visited by an artist with the same question, Franz said, "My dear, the unconscious is so vast that if you worked with me for a lifetime, it would be like dipping a spoon into the ocean.")

I arrived to ask my question. It was about seven o'clock on a humid summer's evening. Strasberg was making himself his usual coffee in a small soup bowl, stirring together twelve spoonfuls of instant coffee, heavy cream, and boiling water. He seated me at the farthest end of his living room. This is how I recall his reply: "Analysis, analysis, yes yes." Snuffle, snuffle. (He had some kind of a nasal problem, which the editors actually cut out of his amazing performance as Hyman Roth in *The Godfather*.) "Yes, yes. Analysis. I remember talking with Franchot [Tone]. When was that? I think it was June, the last year of the Group Theater. No, the year before. I was taking Franchot to Grand Central Station. The Group was running out of money. Yes, yes. He was catching the Twentieth Century Limited to go to Hollywood." Snuffle, snuffle. "I had mixed feelings about that—very, very mixed feelings—was he abandoning the Group? Yes, yes." Snuffle, snuffle.

It went on like that for a long time. It grew dark outside his great Central Park West windows. I had not said a word. He had not answered my question. Finally, as on that awful day at the Actors Studio, embarrassed and awkward, I snuck out of the room.

I NEVER VISITED STRASBERG AGAIN, but I heard many years later that he had his own transformative experience at Radio City Music Hall. Every year, Radio City held an extravaganza called the Night of a Thousand Stars. On Valentine's Day 1982, Strasberg, as his part of the entertainment, joined Al Pacino and Robert De Niro for a vigorous kick line with the Rockettes. He left the stage and died three days later.

8

I WAS WORKING as a stage manager at the Actor's Workshop in San Francisco in 1960. I had moved there, inspired by the radical vision of that theater's directors, Herbert Blau and Jules Irving. A college friend phoned from New York to say he couldn't find the money to back a play he was producing: *The Blacks* by the French writer, activist, and criminal Jean Genet. Would I invest in the project and join in as a producer? I read it, got into the car with Chiquita, pregnant with our first child, and our Scottish terriers, and headed east. The play opened Off Broadway in 1961, a week before my twenty-seventh birthday.

The play was a success. *The Blacks* ran for more than 1,400 performances. The cast featured James Earl Jones, Roscoe Lee Browne, Cicely Tyson, Godfrey Cambridge, Louis Gossett, and, believe it or not, Maya Angelou. I met Genet, even went out with him once for coffee. The only coffee he'd ever tasted that was as bad as American coffee, he told me, was in a French prison.

9

I HAD BEGUN A LIFE in the theater. After the success of *The Blacks*, and with almost no directing experience, I got hired by a man named Stuart Vaughan to be associate artistic director at the newly established Seattle Repertory Theatre for its first season.

Vaughan and I were oil and water. I found him pedantic and academic, and he must have found me to be trouble. He opened the season—and the theater—with *King Lear*, followed by my production of Max Frisch's *Firebugs*, a political satire about the rise of Hitler and bourgeois complacency. In the play, two clown-faced arsonists, pretending to be traveling salesmen—obviously Hitler and Goebbels—talk their way into houses all over town. The pyromaniacs go door to door, setting attic fires everywhere, but the townspeople still refuse to believe that evil can come to them. A mock Greek chorus of firemen chants: "Call us in. Call us in."

I didn't really know what I was doing, so I felt my way forward, tentatively. I sent the chorus to a local school for firemen to learn how firemen hold the hoses. (We found out they do it differently in different cities.) It gave them a style, an extraordinary look. My staging of the ending was quite theatrical. As the town is going up in flames, an actual fire engine drove onto the stage. A large round trampoline was lowered from the fly loft, and films of the atomic bombing of Hiroshima were projected onto it. The proscenium arch was covered with blow-ups of newsprint articles about Seattle scandals that had been swept under the rug. The engine ladders, swarming with firemen, swung out over the auditorium. The firemen threw handfuls of confetti. Doris Day sang "Que Sera Sera."

I was fired.

I had just turned thirty.

BACK IN NEW YORK we lived with our son, Nick—our daughter, Marina, was about to be born—in a tiny apartment in one of those ugly, generic brick Manhattan high-rises that popped up like inedible mushrooms in New York after World War II. All my friends were leftovers from years in WASPy prep schools, WASPy Harvard, and family summers in WASPy East Hampton.

For my birthday, Chiquita threw me a surprise party. I walked into our apartment, saw all those WASPs raising glasses of champagne, singing happy birthday, and I thought, *If these are my friends, I'm fucked.* Two days later I began Freudian analysis. (From then on, I would remain in some sort of therapy for most of the rest of my adult life.) Three years later, despite the analysis, or maybe because of it, I had been thrown out of two more theaters.

Chiquita, still feeling like a stranger in New York, stayed with the children and stood by me through it all.

AS I TRIED to mature as a director, I realized I needed someone to help me on my way. I sought out Alan Schneider. He was a very successful director both in the regional theater and on Broadway, and I admired his avant-garde tastes. He had the chutzpah to direct the American premiere of Samuel Beckett's *Waiting for Godot* at the Coconut Grove Playhouse in Florida, and again, successfully, on Broadway. He premiered Edward Albee's *Who's Afraid of Virginia Woolf?* He also directed the American premiere of Beckett's *Endgame*, which changed my life. So I took him out to lunch. I asked him: "How do I become a director like you?" He said I must create my own theater outside of New York. "How do I do that?" I asked. "That's up to you," he replied.

AT THAT TIME there were very few regional theaters across the country. I bought myself a large map of America, put it up on the wall, pinned a red flag in each good city that already had a theater, a blue flag in lousy cities, and a gold flag in excellent cities with no theater. I came up with Philadelphia.

I SOMEHOW CONVINCED Malcolm Eisenberg, a Philadelphia interior designer, to invest in me after I told him over the phone my vision for the theater. He came away inspired. (In all honesty, I cannot remember what I told him.) He agreed to throw three parties, at which I would talk about my ideas. I went to these parties and asked anyone who was inspired by my talk to find three friends to throw three more parties. Over two years, I talked at nearly 200 events, such as breakfast parties, luncheons, cocktail parties, and dinners. I managed to line up 8,000 subscribers to support a theater that did not exist. Thus, the Theatre of Living Arts was born. Soon, too, was my daughter, Marina.

THE THEATER BEGAN QUIETLY with a decent production of Brecht's *Galileo* (which by now I knew was not *The Fisherman of Galilee*), mounted in only two weeks. I followed with a conventional production of Chekhov's *Uncle Vanya* and a more adventurous production of *Poor Bitos* by Jean Anouilh.

In the second season, however, everything changed. The quiet-spoken, polite-seeming, gentleman André transformed into a wolf-man, raging through his own theater world, vengeful and angry, fire shooting out of his ears. Still angry at my parents, I was bent on destruction. I couldn't battle my parents directly, so instead I was determined to drive my boring, bourgeois subscription audience screaming out of the theater. I was also a young director saying, "Look what I can do! Look what the theater can do!"

A married couple, George Bartenieff and Crystal Field, who would go on to found the experimental Off-Off Broadway stronghold Theatre for the New City in New York's East Village, brought me a play called *Beclch*. The play had everything: sex, cannibalism, filthy language. (Remember, this was the sixties.) It set me on fire. I had to do it.

The board of directors of my theater was totally against doing this, but I smooth-talked them into it, promising that I would never again produce such a play (a promise that inadvertently came true). The president of the board, a charming woman, whose husband headed the CIA, said, "You could talk the Virgin Mary out of *it*."

Beclch is about a housewife, bored to death by her dull life and milquetoast husband, who runs off to an Africa of the subconscious: Africa as it might appear in a white suburbanite's Technicolor wet dream. She travels to this imaginary Africa and, voracious for experience and hungry for adventure, she begins fucking the locals and ends up eating them. Rochelle Owens, who wrote it, had gained notoriety a couple of years earlier with *Futz* at La MaMa, a play about a farmer who makes love to his pig.

I hired an artistic Wild Bunch to help me mount the play: the experimental composer Teiji Ito, who had written music for the Living Theatre; Carolee Schneemann, an environmentalist who was well known on the East Village art scene for her work on sexuality and the body; and the Arthur Hall Afro American Dance Ensemble. Then there was Eugene Lee, who would design nearly all my productions for fifty years and who was even more of an "Angry Young Man" than I was becoming.

The theater was in an inner-city slum. The arriving audience was greeted at the front of the building by two or three Watusi from the Dance Ensemble, each about six and a half feet tall, and led one at a time down a dark and sinister alley. Once backstage, audience members faced a totem pole covered with hundreds of condoms filled with grape juice. They were asked to chop off one of the condoms. After this symbolic act of violence, every spectator received a wooden African mask before being directed to cross the stage, a large mud pit covered by a few wooden paths, and sit down. They sat, still masked, in an auditorium covered with vines—our jungle.

AT THE MOVIES, when shocking things happen, you are protected by darkness. This is why I gave the audience masks—to make them anonymous and protect them from being seen. Also, I wanted to transform them into jungle natives. Teiji Ito's musicians sat in a pit at the center of the mud and played ancient African instruments borrowed from museums.

In the second act, the playwright describes the stage as littered with corpses—animal and human. One of our board members was an executive from Smith Kline & French, the pharmaceutical company that made Contac cold pills, and I asked if he knew a chemist who could create the smell of rotting flesh. He sent one. Did I want the smell of animal or human flesh? the chemist inquired. "Both, ideally." A few days later he showed up with a glass bottle filled with liquid. "Just a few drops in the air-cooling system should do the trick," he said. I was having the time of my life.

At tech rehearsal, the stage manager cued the smell, and we waited. And waited. Suddenly an actor ran offstage and vomited. The putrid smell was so intense it permeated the carpets and upholstery. We had to postpone opening by five days. We kept rehearsing. I got a call from the ASPCA; they were trying to close the production down. You see, Teiji's Haitian musicians had been sacrificing live goats at night against the brick wall behind the theater to bring the production good fortune. I hadn't noticed. I was having too much fun. This was directing!

The most difficult stage direction came in the final act. The main character, to make her husband more of a man, seduces him into undergoing the rite of elephantiasis. The natives of this strange land place huge worms and leeches on his leg. The stage directions call for the leg to grow huge with pus in the vivid colors of a Chagall painting.

How could we get the leg to do that? That's what directors do! That's the magic of directing! I solved the directing problem by *mis*direction. The three upstage haystacks began to move with the pulse of Teiji's wild music, like three huge erections waving back and forth. The dance troupe weaved and swayed, the men wearing nothing but Pepsi-Cola bottle-top penis sheathes and the women covered by little more than election buttons over their nipples. (I told you: It was the sixties.) Swaying haystack erections, wild pulsing music, nearly naked dancers—no one noticed the stagehand who walked onstage and positioned, over the actor's leg, a vivid, Chagall-painted, dummy one.

One of our subscribers, a blue-haired lady paralyzed for twelve years from the waist down, appeared at the theater with her fifty-year-old son. Because she was in a wheelchair, we skipped the sinister alley and brought her through the lobby. When this music-pulsing, haystack-dancing, Pepsi-top-penis-covered mayhem began she became so outraged, so offended, that she rose out of her wheelchair and stormed out of the theater. Her son ran up the aisle after her, shouting "Oh my God! Oh my God! Mommy's walking! Mommy's walking!" The audience thought it was planned. It wasn't. Her son had tried everything to help her to walk—physiotherapy, psychotherapy, shock therapy—everything. He wrote to thank us. My theater of miracles had begun!

THE PLAY OPENED TO TERRIBLE REVIEWS. Our subscribers stayed home. Other than the few African American neighborhood children who came every night, we had a total flop. The board was relieved: They figured nothing like this would ever happen again.

While the play was running, though, a blizzard hit and Ted Kalem, *Time* magazine's theater critic, trying to reach Washington, D.C., to review a play at Arena Stage, got stuck in Philadelphia. He asked the hotel concierge what to see in town. The concierge sent him to us.

Me with Teddy and my brother, Alexis, in
Paris on the brink of war, 1938

In Paris, all
dressed up

Alex and me with
our mother,
1940

A rare glimpse of my father looking happy in Switzerland, 1936

Family portrait, New York

At the Central
Park Zoo, 1943

Only in Hollywood

With Isee at
Choate graduation

Zuylen Castle, and home, in the Netherlands

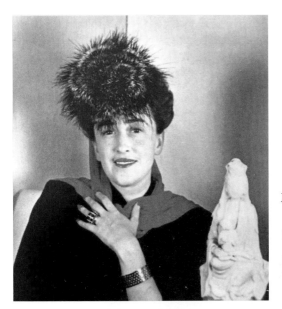

Mother hated
this picture,
but she loved
the hat.

My father
and me, Choate
graduation,
1952

Marriage, '50s style

Chiquita and me at
the Brussels World
Fair, 1958

With my son,
Nicholas

Chiquita with baby Marina

At my first rehearsal of *Galileo* in Philadelphia

Chiquita shooting her first documentary
in the Soviet Union

Ten days later *Time* ran a four-page spread on *Beclch* with pictures. And so, the play, performing in a Philadelphia slum, became a New York hit. Off-Off Broadway audiences poured into Philadelphia. Subscribers, changing their minds after reading *Time*, tried to come back and couldn't get in. We were sold out, a sensation.

The board, predictably, was terrified by this success. They imagined more plays like this one, and me more emboldened to push the envelope. So they fired me.

ANDRÉ GIDE WROTE: "I was more easily disgusted at twenty, and I was less satisfied with life. I embraced less boldly; I breathed less deeply; and I felt myself to be less loved. Perhaps also I longed to be melancholy; I had not yet understood the superior beauty of happiness."

10

I WAS BECOMING an *enfant terrible*, but more importantly—
and more lastingly—I was discovering, as I had with the end of
Firebugs, the unlimited and thrilling theatrical possibilities that
are the director's domain.

But Philadelphia was over. And I had nowhere to go. Who
would hire me? I had been praised as one of the most talented directors to emerge from the new regional theater movement, but
after having been fired yet again, I felt devastated and isolated.
I had worked for three years to fulfill a dream, the creation of a
permanent acting company. And now the dream was shattered.
What I had done in Philadelphia I most probably would never be
able to do again. I was a failure.

Then the phone rang. It was nearly midnight. Who could be calling at this hour?

Gregory Peck.

Gregory Peck?!

The legendary movie star and leader of Hollywood. Atticus Finch himself. Royalty. Why in the world would he be calling me?

Prior to this call, my future was uncertain.

And then Gregory Peck called.

HE TOLD ME that the Department of Health, Education and Welfare, an offshoot of Johnson's Great Society, had funded three theaters to bring fine performances to high school kids and adults in three cities: New Orleans, Providence, and Los Angeles. The first two had already gone under, having failed to reach their audiences. It was L.A.'s turn. He wanted to hire an interracial group of actors to play for the city's black, white, Asian, and Latino students. The theater would work with the school board, but only to choose plays that might appeal to that audience. Peck, who had seen one of my productions in Philadelphia, wanted me to head the L.A. theater. He wanted me! But surely he was mistaken? Maybe there was another André, one better suited, and he had confused us?

"Greg, I'm the guy who dressed a black dance troupe in rosary-bead penis sheathes and campaign button pasties. I could never work with a school board. Besides that, I'm exhausted. You should find someone else."

Unfazed, Peck offered me his house in Acapulco. "If you're exhausted, it's yours. For as long as you like. When you feel better, stop by L.A. for lunch. If your answer is still no—a considered no—then I will accept that."

Just like that, I was the artistic director of an interracial theater in Watts, which had recently been ravaged by riots.

MY FIRST PRODUCTION at the Inner City Cultural Center was Molière's *Tartuffe*. I wanted our production to connect with a broad spectrum of kids, from black kids in Watts, whose parents had to spend a whole day to take the one daily bus out of the neighborhood to pick up their assistance checks, to the white kids from Beverly Hills, who got driven to school in fancy convertibles.

I set the production in an imaginary, Wild West–style Mexico in the 1840s. We taught the actors gunslinging. Orgon, the master of the house, was played as a ranch-owning closet queen. We based him on President LBJ. The handsome young black actor Lou Gossett played Tartuffe, the opportunist who almost cons Orgon out of house, home, and daughter. Our Tartuffe was torn between love of money and love of Orgon's young wife, Elmire, a New Orleans beauty, played by Allyn Ann McLerie, a white actress.

The theater had, once upon a time, been a movie palace, and on its voluminous red velvet curtain we painted the reproduction of a female nude that had once hung in a San Francisco saloon. There is an old French tradition of the stage manger knocking three times before the curtain rises. Instead, we had a Native American woman ride down the aisle on a horse, stand on her saddle, and shoot three times at a real, candlelit chandelier suspended in front of the curtain. While a small Mexican-American orchestra played "La Cucaracha," the curtain went up in flames. And so *Tartuffe* began.

As we were about to open Peck phoned me to say that some board members, including African Americans, were opposed to our black Tartuffe kissing the white Elmire. The kiss would have to go. (This same year, *Guess Who's Coming to Dinner*, featuring a black doctor, played by Sidney Poitier, preparing to marry the white daughter of the Katharine Hepburn and Spencer Tracy characters, was playing all over town.) Scratch the surface of the seemingly sophisticated Los Angeles, I discovered, and you find an Oklahoma backwater. Philadelphia-like conflict was simmering, so I took the kiss out. With no touching, the scene was fueled by suppressed desire—even more erotic. When the play opened, the shit hit the fan. Outraged parents picketed the school board. The Catholic Church stamped the production with its "seal of condemnation." The reviews were awful. The only people who seemed to like it were the school kids and Eldridge Cleaver, the Black Panther leader. "I'm gonna call it Tar-tough because it's tough enough for me," he told me after one performance.

PECK CALLED ME to a meeting with "the bitch on the hill," which is what everyone called the superintendent of the school board. She had given herself the nickname because her office was on a hill, and she was a self-proclaimed bitch. At the meeting were Peck, me, the school board's lawyer, the L.A. sheriff, and the bitch (who was tougher than the sheriff). I was only thirty-two years old and scared. We were planning Brecht's *Caucasian Chalk Circle* as our second offering, and the "B.O.T.H." told us we couldn't do it. She'd been swamped with letters calling the Marxist Brecht a "dirty commie." To avoid trouble, I agreed to substitute Tennessee Williams's *The Glass Menagerie*. How could that cause trouble? I would hire a good, non-controversial director at the L.A. branch of the Actors Studio and stay in the background.

I went home to rest.

The director called me. There was only one actor in the company suitable for the role of the Gentleman Caller, and that actor was black. Was that a cause for concern? Let's put the question to the bitch on the hill, I suggested. See if she'd get on the phone and tell us not to do it. Happily, she didn't see any problem with it. The Gentleman Caller didn't have an explicit sexual relationship with anyone. No kissing. The director went into rehearsal, and I went back home to rest.

About three weeks later, close to opening, Peck called to say that Tennessee Williams had heard that we'd cast a black actor and was outraged. He demanded that we recast the role. Tennessee outraged, about a black actor? I couldn't believe it. I phoned his agent, the venerable Audrey Wood, but as a young and unknown director I couldn't get through to her. Though it was unusual (and expensive) at that time, I booked a flight for the long trip to New York.

I got in to see Miss Wood. She was surprised when I told her why I was there. Tennessee would never give a damn about such a thing. Also, he was on an African safari and couldn't possibly have heard about the casting. By the time I got back to L.A., Wood had sent my board a telegram saying something like: "Any actor can do any play of mine out of New York regardless of race, creed or color. Good luck. Tennessee Williams."

There was a limo waiting at the airport. Waiting for me? Yes, to take me to George Cukor's house for lunch. I'd seen many of Cukor's movies, but had never met him. He was way out of my league. He had worked with many of the great legends of the time, Bette Davis, Greta Garbo, Marilyn Monroe. Why would the great Cukor invite me to lunch? This was getting strange.

We sat together by his pool drinking martinis. Before lunch he took me on a tour of his collection of Impressionist paintings.

After lunch, over Cuban cigars, he said: "Now look, André. I know you didn't come to L.A. to direct plays. And you know I know. No one comes here to do that. You want a movie and we'll get you a movie. Just get rid of the black guy."

My reply: "You know what, Mr. Cukor? I've always been a great fan of yours. But fuck you." And with that I hitchhiked home, determined to quit. By the time I got home it was late, and there was a message from Peck. He had found a great solution to the black actor problem, he thought. Greg requested the pleasure of my company early the next morning at Columbia Pictures. I decided to give this one more chance before quitting. Besides, I'd never visited a major studio.

The guard at the gate directed me to Makeup. Once there I found my unfortunate Gentleman Caller in a red wig and white-face. That was the end! Whatever was going on with these people, I wanted no more of it.

I called Peck and asked for a meeting. We sat in his luxurious, tasteful library. He gave me a Perrier (maybe the first I'd ever seen in the States).

We fell into a heated argument. "You know your problem?" he snapped. "You're so overindulgent with your actors that they give rotten performances." I replied, arrogantly, "And your problem, Greg, is that you never had a director like me. If you had, you might have become a real actor instead of a wooden Indian!" With that he slugged me.

Peck was in his fifties then and quite tall. Bleeding slightly, I returned home and called the airlines. Another regional theater, another disaster. First Seattle, then Philadelphia, and now Los Angeles. Three strikes. I was out.

. . .

A COUPLE OF YEARS LATER I told my story to an arts reporter from *Women's Wear Daily*. He wanted to write a piece about my experience, but I wouldn't let him. My name was already mud in the theater. Without my permission the reporter did some nosing around. Here's what he found: It happened that Peck was a very good friend of LBJ's. The president often invited him to the White House and would pick him up in *Air Force One*. The reporter's theory: Johnson wanted to run Peck for governor of California, but in order to do so, he would need support from the "minorities." Hence, his leadership and the interracial board of the Inner City Cultural Center. It seems far-fetched, I know. But if it's true, by crashing and burning in Watts, by destroying Peck's theater, I ruined his chance of becoming governor. Reagan became the governor instead. Without Reagan we might have had no Bush, no war in Iraq, and no Trump. If this reporter's theory is true—even a little true—I should rot in hell.

TRURO, WHERE I NOW LIVE in the summers, lies on a spit of land sixty miles out to sea. Its beautiful Atlantic beaches are only a mile from bay beaches where the swimming is warmer than in the ocean. Hundreds of freshwater ponds scattered through the woods are even warmer. Mother Nature, pissed and vengeful, is beginning to hit us with everything she's got.

Signs of global warming are right under our noses. The warmer waters drive herds of seals our way, followed by great white sharks. Last weekend, the Labor Day beach crowds watched with horror as another great white killed another seal, a small fountain of blood gushing up out of the waters. Walking the beach I find rotting, half-devoured carcasses, covered with seaweed.

Earlier this summer small, slimy caterpillars carpeted the sand. They had decimated the surrounding trees and were looking for water. We expect them to appear every seven years, but now they arrive every year. Swarms of ticks, too. A fisherman told me that red parasite blobs keep showing up on the skin of local fish, a result of ingesting seal shit. All of this is awful.

11

I WAS THIRTY-THREE and couldn't get a job as dogcatcher. As if flaming out of three theaters and provoking Gregory Peck to slug me weren't bad enough, I had accepted a job to direct a play about bestiality on Broadway. *Leda Had a Little Swan* was, to my knowledge, the first play in Broadway history to close the night before it opened. It also sealed my reputation as a lunatic, an angry young wild man, or, as one critic called me, a "loose cannon," not fit for any civilized theater.

Chiquita and I were living as trust-fund babies. My father had bought our apartment and would put our kids through school. I had an income I didn't earn. Without the pressure to make money, I might have used this time to get closer to Chiquita and our young children. Instead, I spent most of it worrying about my failed career.

The dean of the new Tisch School of the Arts at New York University called out of the blue and asked me to lead a workshop with the school's first class of graduating students. Since I had nothing else to do and, clearly, had no future, I agreed. We worked for six weeks. I liked the kids and, despite considering it somewhat demeaning to squander my "great talents" on students, had a good time. That was late spring, 1968.

WE STARTED WITHOUT A PROJECT IN MIND. We began by training together, armed with only a willingness to improvise and a copy of Jerzy Grotowski's *Towards a Poor Theatre*. Grotowski's recently published book included pictures of his groundbreaking work with the Polish Laboratory Theatre and descriptions of psycho-physical exercises, specifically his Exercises Plastique, a series of gestures and movements, starting with isolations of parts of the body, that work for training actors the way increasingly complicated scales might for musicians.

Together, these graduating students and I, as the Manhattan Project, would create one of the biggest theatrical hits of the decade. Ironically, we had named ourselves after the Manhattan Project, which developed the first nuclear weapons, because in rehearsal we were so sure we would bomb.

Many of the students in my new group had taken a workshop with Grotowski at NYU in '67, the previous semester. I had yet to meet him or see his work. I first heard of Grotowski's work from my mother, who had seen his company at the Spoleto Festival in Italy before he came to the States. Around this time, I had a conversation with Ellen Stewart, the founder and great artistic spirit of La MaMa Experimental Theatre Club. Ellen had seen my production of Rochelle Owens's *Beclch* in Philadelphia, and she told me how exciting she had found the work.

"No, no," I said. "It's not what I'm after. I want an actor who can fly. I want scenery made of human bodies. I don't want stage lights, I want light that emanates from the actor's body."

"You should go and see the work of this young man in Poland," she said. "It might help you on your way."

I didn't need any more encouragement. Over NYU's summer break, I went to Poland.

BUT HE WASN'T THERE. I spent the summer traveling around Europe before going to see his work at the Edinburgh Festival in August. On a hunch I had ordered tickets for twelve nights in a row. The hunch changed my life. The hunch changed my work.

Grotowski's play was *Acropolis*. The first night I went with Eugene Lee, my set designer friend. We had never seen anything like this. It was a work of theater that looked as if it had been created by Michelangelo. It was so far ahead of anything we could ever imagine doing that we stayed up all night in my hotel, finishing a bottle of bourbon and vowing to leave the theater. I went back every night, and every night I left a note for Grotowski, asking if we could meet. All day I would wait at my hotel for an answer. No answer came until the day of their last performance. The note said, "I have a press conference this afternoon before the performance, very little time, but we could talk for a few minutes." And it was a short talk, a very short talk. With just moments to introduce myself to him, I could only think to describe the nudity in *Beclch*.

When I returned to the States all I could think about and all I could talk about was this theater miracle that I had seen. Grotowski. Grotowski. Grotowski. I bored friends with this word, "Grotowski."

THEATER, THE MOST EPHEMERAL of all the arts, exists, transformed, in our memories. It can be impossible to describe, but I'm going to give it a shot, because I want you to see what I saw in Scotland. The actor's instrument is the self, the body and voice, the depth of emotional expression. I'd compare a competent actor's instrument to, maybe, a good banjo, which is all right, because many plays are written for actor-banjos. Each Polish Lab actor, as physically expressive as a great dancer, was closer to a Stradivarius. They were trained to express with every part of their bodies. You could not know what an actor's ankle was "saying," but it would vibrate or resonate in some part of your (the audience's) unconscious. Like an unnoticed cello or flute in an orchestral symphony. Their voices, too, were more than sublime. We are used to being reached in performance by words, but these actors' chants or nonverbal sounds were as clear and precise as any words. The performances were poems in action—the poetry of a spiritual existence.

The "story" of one production I later saw concerned a prince, persecuted by the Church, who is transformed by his torturers into a saint. The atmosphere of the small room, the theater, was somber, monastic, and slightly sinister. (Grotowski's work generally was so dark, so medieval and transgressive, that one prominent Parisian theater critic warned readers to stay away, as the work could make them physically ill.)

There was a moment near the end that, each time I saw it, left me literally breathless, as though I'd been kicked in the stomach. The "saint," or Constant Prince of the title, overwhelmed by his persecutors, would faint. This faint took a little longer than a "realistic" faint, but just a little. From standing he would slip to the ground, grab the long hair on his head, strike the head hard, three times on the floor, and die.

I once asked Jerzy why this moment was so powerful. If you filmed it, he told me, and slowed it down, you would find twelve separate physical moments—twelve Stations of the Cross—each born out of years of rehearsal. Each of these imperceptible "stop-action" moments reflected a moment of "confession," the confession of personal secrets buried so deeply in the actor's psyche that, until the work began, even he didn't know existed. By the time he reached the floor, by the time he "died," he was completely purged, an empty shell. The "corpse," wearing only a loincloth, his body as beautiful as a Donatello statue, was lifted onto a wooden plank, as the performance came to an end and our tiny audience (witnesses, Grotowski called us) filed past and out of the theater. He was no longer breathing. He wasn't *pretending* not to breathe; the life had gone out of him. This control had taken years to accomplish. (Didn't Christ, expiring on the cross, cry out, "It is accomplished"?) We, the witnesses, weren't impressed; we were stunned. The theater was a place of miracles, and Grotowski's work was as fully *alive* as theater can be.

12

ONE NIGHT IN NEW YORK, during the rough, uncertain early days of the Manhattan Project, the telephone rang at three in the morning and a foreign voice that sounded vaguely familiar said that he was doing a workshop and would I like to join. I followed my hunch. "Yes. When does it begin?" I asked. "Tomorrow," he answered. "Is it at NYU?" "No," he said. "It's in Aix en Provence."

I had thrown out my back, probably from the stress of my successive failures. I went to our family doctor and asked him if I could go to Europe. I told him about the strenuous exercises I most likely would be doing there. "Are you mad?" he responded.

"You have a family. You can't risk your body by going and doing something that insane."

I was heartbroken. As I walked along the street I came across a movie theater that was showing *Yellow Submarine*. I went in to watch the movie and figure out what to do next. I was so thrilled by *Yellow Submarine* that I thought to myself, "If the Beatles can do this, then I can go to Europe." That night I was on a plane.

When I arrived in Aix I went to my hotel. I waited for the elevator to take me up to my room. The elevator door opened and there, like Pirandello's Six Characters, appeared the members of the Polish Lab Theatre looking like a motorcycle gang—cropped hair, black leather jackets and boots. I was looking at the face of Soviet Eastern Europe and at the greatest acting company in the world.

Our first session began in a darkened rehearsal room at one in the morning. We sat on metal chairs, the only light from a gooseneck lamp on an aluminum tabletop. The lamp cast an eerie glow on the faces of the greatest theater director in the world and the greatest actor since Eleonora Duse. Not that they needed a special light to make them seem odd. Grotowski, pasty-faced and rolypoly, wore a black suit, with starched shirt, black tie, and dark sunglasses. Ryszard Cieslak, his trained body looking like a Rodin sculpture, had the largest eyes I have ever seen. Later I heard the story behind these eyes, a story of fanatical devotion.

Cieslak had been dissatisfied with his eyes. He found them too close and squinty, what in the fifties we used to call "bedroom eyes." He felt that the eyes are the windows to the soul, and the work of the Lab was filled with soul. So everywhere the company went, he tried to find a surgeon who could make his eyes larger. But this is impossible.

In India, though, he met a man in a tiny village in the country. The man said that if you roll your eyes around the edge of the moon every night of the full moon every month of the year for years, your eyes will get larger. But be sure to keep wiping butter on the lids, he cautioned. If you don't, they will crack. Cieslak did just that for three or four years. He created for himself the enormous eyes I was now staring into. They were like the eyes of a carp.

We worked most of that first night. Excruciatingly difficult exercises that took enormous stamina and enormous courage. The worst of all were tiger leaps. Cieslak would kneel on the floor and raise his arms in a V over his head, and you would have to run toward him, leap over his head between his raised arms, and do a somersault. I was terrified. I did not like to be disoriented. I did not like to be upside down. I was sure that as I leapt toward him, my head would crack open against his. We were also doing the Exercises Plastiques, developed by Grotowski and Eugenio Barba, and my God, could Grotowski's actors move! Each one could move twenty or thirty muscles in the face alone, so there was no barrier between an emotional impulse and the physical expression of that impulse.

The exercises divided every part of the body into about forty separate gestures or notes, so that you could have a conversation with yourself or with another, a conversation of movements, of gestures. The actor starts with his first impulse, maybe circles made by his head, and follows that impulse until it runs out or a new impulse takes over. You could create a poem of the self, not aesthetic, but moving from the subconscious to a gesture on the surface, reflecting the passions, the turbulent rhythms flowing below the surface, opening the imagination through physical commitment. This was truly a "Song of Myself."

These exercises moved the actor away from a theater that was primarily verbal. By committing unused parts of the body, by dissolving physical blocks, you dissolved fears, developed courage, and released from the body emotions that had been kept on ice for decades. Watching them, I knew they had the potential to release me as well. Grotowski's exercises proved essential for my training of the Manhattan Project actors. I wanted an actor who could fly. I got an actor who could fly. And I found the teacher who had the technical key with which I could train that actor to fly.

During those first few days so very long ago, each one of which I approached with dread, I only remember Grotowski saying three or four memorable things. The most memorable was this: An actor asked what he should primarily work toward. Grotowski answered, "*Sincérité in extremis, mais les détails en cristal*," which in English means what it sounds like: sincerity at its most extreme, but details in crystal. This "*extremis*" also refers to the moments before death.

Perhaps I was afraid and, on some deep level, sensed this workshop was taking me into a strange and unknown future. (It was.) Perhaps the exercises were too arduous for me. (They weren't.) Perhaps I feared opening the Pandora's box of feelings I held in my body. (I did.) Whatever the reasons, I found the workshop tedious and uninteresting. I found Grotowski pretentious.

Having not yet learned that boredom—in therapy or in rehearsal—is often a sign of avoidance, sharks in the water you don't want to face, I decided to withdraw from the workshop. I felt I owed him the respect to tell him so in person. I asked him if we could have dinner together. That would be delightful, he said, as he needed a translator for an article he was sending to *The New York Times*. *He's not only pretentious*, I thought; *he's also condescending. He's treating me like his secretary.*

At dinner we talked a lot about our childhoods. We drank cheap hot wine and brandy. (He was trying to kill a cold.) We got so drunk that we ended up in a tiny square at dawn in front of a fountain, trying unsuccessfully to levitate. We said good night. I went back to my hotel, fell into a deep sleep, and had the following dream:

I was in a kind of garden of Eden, walking with Grotowski and the other members of the workshop. We were having an amazing discussion of Nietzsche and Dostoyevsky. One by one the others in the group disappeared till finally there was only him and me.

He said to me: "I am going into a burning desert. Would you like to come with me? You don't have to."

At which I found myself up on the balcony of a skyscraper, one leg caught in a bicycle wheel, desperately clutching my working script for *The Bacchae*, which I was supposed to direct at Yale. As I tried to free my leg, frightened of my precious work script falling over the edge and dizzy from the height I was about to plunge, the window opened. At the window were Joseph and the Virgin Mary.

Joseph said to me: "If you come in and make love to Mary, we will give you sanctuary." After this act of love, which I cannot remember, Joseph injected a hypodermic needle into Mary's arm and, very peacefully, she died.

Because of this act of love and this act of death, I found myself back with my teacher. Grotowski put on my head and shoulders the furs of the princes of all the Russias. I felt my body growing strong and large and powerful. Hand in hand, with the furs on my head and my shoulders, Grotowski and I walked into the burning desert . . .

When I awoke I felt transformed. I was filled with energy, strength, and a courage I had never known. I didn't leave. On the contrary, I came back into the workshop like a kamikaze. I did extraordinary work. I couldn't even believe this was *me*. Who was this André Gregory? When the workshop in Provence ended and we parted, I vomited for two days. The umbilical cord that joined me to my teacher had been cut. What would I do without him?

13

I HAD COME TO THE WORKSHOP in Provence ready, upon my return to the States, to dissolve the Manhattan Project. Our company seemed chaotic and amateurish. But when I returned to New York, I entered into the work with renewed energy and passion.

WE WERE INSPIRED by Grotowski's "poor theater" principles: Since the theater cannot compete with the visual magic of film, it must find what is unique to itself. To do so, we asked what the theater can do *without*. It can do without lights and sets and costumes and music. All it needs is one actor and one spectator.

So the *Alice* group set out to create the whole of Lewis

Carroll's world with no tricks—only a long table and a single, strong light. No scenery. We would make magic with six actors and our imaginations, six actors performing dozens of roles— White Rabbit, Humpty Dumpty, Jabberwock, Cheshire Cat, and many more. Tables, keys, doors, croquet balls and wickets. Whatever we needed, the actors would become. They would transform from one character to another in front of our eyes without makeup or new costumes.

How can an actor transform himself into a caterpillar, with no change of costume or makeup, and then sit on a mushroom that isn't there? How can a child be turned into a pig? How can a sweet-faced White Queen, daffy and angelic, suddenly become a Red Queen, ugly and mean, dangerous and full of fury—one actress but totally different people? We wanted magic: if a magician can saw a woman in half . . .

We took both Lewis Carroll books, *Alice's Adventures in Wonderland* and *Through the Looking Glass*, and chose a handful of chapters and events from which to work, containing characters with whom we deeply identified: "Down the Rabbit Hole," "A Caucus-Race and a Long Tale," "Alice Changes Her Shape," "Advice from a Caterpillar," "Pig and Pepper," "A Mad Tea-Party," "The Queen's Croquet-Ground," "Humpty Dumpty," "The White Knight," and "Alice Goes Back Up the Rabbit Hole." We were drawn to sections that presented impossible theatrical challenges, challenges that could easily be met with the help of a film camera, lights, and sets, but which were totally unrealizable on a bare stage hiding nothing from the audience.

For example, Alice has to fall down a hole, a hole that, on a stage with no scenery, isn't there. How does she do that? How does Alice grow larger and smaller in front of your eyes without light tricks? And, of course, if she falls down a nonexistent rabbit hole, she must fall backward up the hole at the end of the play! *Alice* was a play about the terrors of childhood made real through the imaginations of a bunch of grown-ups who had never grown up. We were like children who turn over a card table and then totally believe it's a pirate ship. "Look, pirates!"

We didn't care about the *story*. We cared about the elements of Carroll's books that turned us on. We wanted to make theater about theater, the way action painting is about the event of painting, the way a circus is about the *acts*. We didn't ask ourselves what tied the events together until the very end of the rehearsal and creation process, two years in. Even then we found only the most artificial connective tissue between scenes, a tissue that gave the *illusion* of a story: Alice, a nice, repressed young girl, on the whim of the moment goes down a rabbit hole only to be battered and confused, to have her mind fucked with by an endless array of sadistic grown-ups.

Charles Dodgson, aka Lewis Carroll, created the book while out punting on the River Thames with the little Liddell sisters. "Tell us a story! Tell us a story!" the sisters cried. And he did. He invented the whole thing with its parade of characters and twisty riddles and ever-changing scenes right off the top of his head, one balmy boating afternoon. As soon as he got home he wrote it all down so he wouldn't forget. In that way the roots of Carroll's great book were sunk deep in his vast unconscious. It was his dream. Our production, likewise, took root in the soil of the company's unconscious. It grew from places and in ways we could never rationally explain. It was our collective dream.

ONE OF THE PROBLEMS of making a play from *Alice*—especially if, like me, you had spent years at the Actors Studio, where there is a constant emphasis on psychological truth—is that the world

Carroll describes is completely crazy. It's apparently *illogical*, but to make it work onstage you have to find logic in the illogic. You have to create the reality of each scene.

For instance, Alice walks into a mad tea party:

(*At this point the tableau around the table comes to life and the Hatter slams his fist down on the table, shouting:*)
HATTER: NO ROOM. NO ROOM. (*Both Alice and the Cat jump off the table and run.*)
HARE: No, no, no, no . . . no room there; there's room here. (*Taps place by him.*)
HATTER: No room . . . no . . .
ALICE: There's plenty of room . . .

In order to create the reality and subtext of that scene, you have to ask why the Hatter says, "NO ROOM. NO ROOM." You have to ask: In what way is each of the characters mad? How did they go mad? Who were they before they went mad? What is their relationship to one another? How long have they been at that table? What is their relationship to this young girl? And where is Alice coming from? If you don't find the reality under the mayhem, then all you have is a cartoon.

To answer these questions, we did improvisations that went on for months. Sometimes a single improvisation lasted all night. We worked on the tea party without Alice. We rehearsed with only the three men sitting at that table doing whatever they felt like doing or nothing at all. The rule was that they could not go to the bathroom to pee. I had a teapot in which they could do that. The teapot was their toilet.

They sat and they sat and they sat. Month after month after month. "We just sat at that table until the three of us literally went crazy," Larry Pine, who played the Dormouse in that scene, told an interviewer at the time. The improvisation grew scatological, worse than anything you could hear coming out of a marine's mouth. It turned pornographic, and the men acted out incredible fantasies, because there were no women. It became a prison scene. When Alice finally arrived, it was as if somebody had delivered to their prison cell a glorious, magnificent gift. But having been alone so long, they are afraid of their own impulses, what they might do to this girl. "No room! No room!"

Alice seems to be an innocent, who follows a white rabbit down into a world of madness, mayhem, and cruelty, what Ted Kalem of *Time* would call "a vertiginous descent into a laughing hell."

AS WE WORKED, THOUGH, Alice's descent into hell became, for me, a descent into my own childhood. *Alice* is a dream play, but that dream is almost a documentary of my childhood, an insane world filled with weak men trying to fuck up a kid's brain. I was still in Freudian analysis throughout these years, which, being Freudian, focused on childhood. Childhood, childhood, childhood. The analyst was a warm and kind man, and though I almost never saw his face, he gave me an invaluable psychological key with which to unlock this extremely peculiar and elusive text: He showed me how to unravel a dream. From him I learned about dream logic, which is the logic of Lewis Carroll's masterpiece.

THE MANHATTAN PROJECT was its own kind of family, with intense love, sibling rivalries, chronic squabbles, and power dynamics. We avoided the very issues that would ultimately break us apart. But in these early years we lived in a world of our own, both family and friends to one another. Rehearsal was a playground for happy, demented, manic kids, a playground without adult supervision. Showing up each day was like attending the world's most inspired and insane kindergarten.

MY MEMORIES OF THE *ALICE* rehearsals are more vivid than those of my life at home with Chiquita and our two young children, Nicholas and Marina. In this way, maybe I was a product of my time, the father whose mind was always in his work, whether present at home or not, always directing, whether I was in the studio or not, always dreaming of being the new Stanislavski. Certainly I was putting a lot of energy into undoing the damage of my own childhood, using the madness of *Alice* to untangle my own family's madness. I would leave the cozy, bourgeois Upper West Side apartment that Chiquita made home, say goodbye to the doorman, and take the subway downtown to the grungy, Bohemian East Village and the classroom NYU had given us to rehearse in. Uptown, I'm a happy hubby headed for the office; downtown I'm Bob Dylan. Meanwhile, Nicholas and Marina were living through childhoods of their own, cared for mostly by Chiquita, who suffered silently. Or so I believe. She never told me.

IN MANY OF MY WORKS for the theater, and in *My Dinner with André*, I would push as close to madness as possible without falling over the edge. Sometimes I knew this was what I was doing; sometimes it was unconscious. I assumed I was destined for crazy like my depressed father. In the theater I could play with that question, dance on that edge. Whether the actors knew it or not, whether audiences saw it or not, *Alice* was my family portrait, my own descent into their unique lunacy. From that point on, every production I directed would feel autobiographical to me, an attempt to make something artistic out of my life, to better understand myself.

TO OUR AMAZEMENT *Alice* ran for four years, toured the world, and was hailed as one of the Hallmark productions of the 1970s, along with Peter Brook's *A Midsummer Night's Dream* and Grotowski's own work. If John Gruen, an art critic who wrote about *Alice* in *Vogue*, is any indication, our debt to Grotowski and to the madness of my childhood both shone through:

> Imagine an *Alice* played in the manner of Jerzy Grotowski— an *Alice* in which six actors (playing interchangeable roles) writhe, scream, pound, jump, run, and contort themselves until every sinew of their collective body is strained and stretched to a painful point of no return. Consider an *Alice* with a minimum of props—an *Alice* in which total economy of setting, lighting, makeup, and costuming actually *adds* to a production clearly designed to allow language and the orchestration of the body to ignite the imagination.
>
> Watching this *Alice in Wonderland* is an unnerving experience. It disturbs memory and releases certain impulses reaching back to childhood. We are made to reconsider the dream that was our youth. Was it not essentially monstrous? Or did it contain a poetry we were ill-equipped to fathom? Was it all lies or was it all magic? André Gregory goes to *Alice* as to a sorceress in whose deeds, actions, and words might be found some mystic solution.

. . .

OF THE MANY PLACES WE PLAYED, my favorite was at the Shiraz Festival in Iran. We had been assigned space in a television studio rumored to belong to SAVAK, the Iranian secret police. I didn't want to know. We had not come all the way to Iran to perform in an antiseptic TV studio. Besides, who could say what unspeakable crimes had been cleaned away before we arrived? We had to find a different venue.

I asked the festival for a car, and our designer, Eugene Lee, and I traveled all over the old city to find a suitable space. We found the perfect one—an onion and garlic packing factory in a working-class suburb, surrounded by a low brick wall with a large tree bursting through the cement in the middle of what would become the playing area. The audience would sit on fruit crates covered with Persian carpets. The neighborhood children could perch on the walls or in the tree to watch.

This was unusual, because the festival had been created by the wife of the shah, the empress, and her jet-set friends from around the world made up most of the audience. The possibility of revolution was ever present, but the shah's people mistakenly thought that such a revolution would come from the left. The military would only promise adequate protection for the empress for two nights, so she made a deal with the military that she would only go to the festival's opening and closing nights. Ours was not one of those. She must have heard that *Alice* was good, because one afternoon as the actors and I were sitting around this gorgeous space, two Parisian interior decorators showed up with a sofa and a Louis XV coffee table that they placed in front of the fruit crates. When I tried to return to my hotel before the performance, I found that the roads and houses in every direction had been emptied. The empty streets were too ominous to travel. We stayed put.

Two hours before the beginning of the play buses filled with secret police showed up at the space. They wore black glasses and carried black attaché cases filled, I presume, with guns. They set up a submachine gun on the wall and another one backstage. Larry Pine was so terrified that when he made his first entrance, he ran offstage to vomit and came right back. Every member of the audience entering the space was body searched, some taken into a little booth for a rectal inspection.

Secret police were seated everywhere, one for every two members of the audience. In our desire to play Iran some of us had denied the obvious, but now it was brutally clear: that we had landed in the midst of a terrible dictatorship. The empress sat on the sofa with two ladies-in-waiting. After the performance she invited the company to her summer palace. We sat on a balcony, overlooking an artificial pond on which had been constructed a little wooden stage, where folk dancers performed for us alone. We smoked Havana cigars and ate golden caviar, caviar reserved specially for the empress. There was a large desert moon.

Angela (our Alice) introduced her husband, and the empress asked if he was also an actor. "No, I'm an architect." "Oh," she sighed with what seemed like regret. "I trained at the Sorbonne. If I hadn't married a shah, I would have become an architect."

14

MY FREUDIAN ANALYST helped me understand dreams and the psychological logic of human behavior, but he didn't prepare me for how bewildering and disorienting the thrill of a New York hit can be. Journalists write articles about you and magazines want interviews. Famous strangers invite you for dinner.

We followed *Alice* with a production of Samuel Beckett's *Endgame*, a play I had staged in Philadelphia and again to open the first season of the Yale Repertory Theatre in New Haven. In fact, I would revisit the play—or you could say, keep working on it—for forty years. *Endgame* built on the success of *Alice*. Clive Barnes of

The New York Times considered it triumphant, calling it "a lovely production. Even more it is a loving production . . . one of the best things in the American theater here and now." And he dubbed thirty-nine-year-old me "one of the most interesting and innovative directors in the world."

I couldn't believe my own praise. It confused me.

IN THE EARLY SEVENTIES the author Renata Adler had recommended Wallace Shawn to me as a possible translator for Ibsen's *Peer Gynt*. Renata had introduced Wally to our work, and he had come night after night to see *Alice*. He looked to me like a poet, but he was in fact a playwright, having written a number of still unproduced plays. So I commissioned him to write a modern adaptation of Ibsen's *Peer Gynt*. He watched us rehearse the conventional translation for many months, disappeared for months more, and returned with a play called *Our Late Night*, based on our rehearsals. In place of Ibsen's marathon poetic drama, he'd written a one-and-a-half-hour play that takes place at a New York City cocktail party.

The problem with the play—not for me but for some of the actors—was the content: a volcanic outpouring of sexual imagery that never stopped. Ever. Wally's brilliant comedic device replaced the usual cocktail party talk with what the characters were really thinking. For example, in place of, "What do you think about what's going on in Syria?" someone would say, "Gee, I'd really like to lick your tits."

Half of the actors in the Manhattan Project were Catholics with a rigid sense of right and wrong, of what should or should not be said in front of an audience. Some of the company loved the characters they were playing; the others resisted the play like crazy. They just didn't want to do it.

GROTOWSKI WAS IN NEW YORK and needed a tie, so I took him to Bloomingdale's. I complained about the actors, about how exhausted and frustrated I was. "I'm going through the same thing myself," he admitted. "I'm thinking of trying to find a way to dissolve the company. Nicely. Why don't you find a way to do the same?" I couldn't do it, and neither could he.

WE OPENED IN NEW YORK in 1975 to good reviews and a terrifying audience response. One spectator actually got out of his seat and hit Larry Pine. People would shout at the characters from the audience: "Shut the fuck up!" Wally, I think, while delighted to see a play of his done in New York and liking the production, found the experience almost sickening, mostly unpleasant, and even harrowing. He wasn't the only one. Many of the actors agreed. They hated the play and resented me for making them do it.

15

AND THEN, one day in 1975 there we were, the whole company and I, sullen and silent and scared, gathered in a lawyer's office, settling our divorce. As I looked around the circle, I had few friends left. Gerry Bamman, *Alice*'s White Knight, had done more than anyone to keep the company going, and, despite his air of resignation and even boredom, I knew he was still on my side. Angela Pietropinto—Alice herself and the person who'd come up with the idea of adapting *Alice*—looked like someone at her own child's funeral. I knew Angela was still my friend, and I felt she was heartbroken. Saskia Hegt was Dutch and had joined the company just as we started rehearsing *Alice*. Always the outsider, she had toughed her way in and kept at it. She, too, believed in me, though none of it showed on her face. Even Larry Pine, whom I'd continue to work with for decades, looked like he'd rather jump off the top of the Empire State Building than sit there, like he wanted nothing to do with any of us.

Among the people arrayed against me, it was hard to fathom the depth of their anger. Their normally expressive actor faces looked masked—bored, veiled, and dead. One after another they had closed themselves to me. Even our lawyer seemed to resent me.

At that moment, I disliked them all. *They don't care about Art*, I was thinking. *They probably never did.* Behind their masks they were probably thinking: *Oh, it's easy for him to talk about Art with a capital A with his father the businessman picking up the tab. I can't even afford to send my kid to a good school!*

THE MANHATTAN PROJECT had eight long years of mind-bending fun—not work but inspired play—days filled with laughter. We'd been experimental globetrotters. And suddenly, or so it seemed, the party was over. The fun and magic were gone, replaced by arguments and resentment. Once we'd opened Wally's play at the Public Theater, we would sit in a circle, day after day, in a cavernous, uninviting gray room at the Public with little to say and less to do. We couldn't agree on anything, including what play to rehearse next.

Companies like ours in America have a very short life span, usually eight or ten years at best. A like-minded group of artists with a common goal, banding and staying together, can seem like heaven on earth. In practice, though, it has its dark side. Family grievances compound, year after year. The director/father is too often away or too aloof. Brother envies brother. *He doesn't like* my *work and gives* her *all the best roles.* These grievances, unspoken, fester and grow. One day in Paradise, a large, venomous worm appears, burrowing in that once-golden apple.

There were good reasons for the company's breakup, beyond Wally's play and our difficulty communicating. The experimental theater of the sixties was biting the dust. The actors were getting older fast, getting married, having children. They had to make a living. The actors didn't have the economic security that I had. They didn't have international businessmen for fathers. As the seventies wore on, the economy got tougher. Also, the huge success of *Alice* had given some in the company the illusion not only that our success could be repeated, though it never was, but that with more success would come more money and security.

I had not been in group therapy at that time, so I had not learned how to talk openly about problems in a group. The problems got worse. Half of the group was smoking a lot of pot. I was becoming more distant, withdrawn, and aloof. I didn't know what to do. When you can't find a way to speak unpleasant truths, relationships begin to stagnate or sour. I remember walking with Wally's father, William Shawn, the iconic editor of *The New Yorker*, the day we evacuated South Vietnam. "Thank God it's over," I said. "It's only beginning," he replied. What did he mean? "Well, you know what happens in families when you sweep all the garbage under the carpet? That's what we are going to do, and it will return to sting us." And he was right.

I SHALL NEVER FORGET that awful hour and a half in a lawyer's office when we, who been such great friends and colleagues, simply, quietly, officially called it quits. We had performed for years.

We had led workshops everywhere, rehearsed almost every day of every month of every year, and now the unimaginable had happened. How did we get here? Where did we go wrong? How could this happen? It really was a marriage, coming apart at the seams. When you're young and in love, you can't imagine your divorce, any more than when you're young you can imagine your death.

BEFORE WE LEFT the lawyer's office, I read from Harold Clurman's *The Fervent Years*, his final words about the demise of the Group Theatre, maybe the most important company in the history of the American theater. What the hell was I doing? Who the hell did I think I was, holding forth, intoning the words of a theater pioneer eulogizing his dead, great theater. Needless to say, no one was impressed.

Why couldn't I have, instead, said something like, "I have loved you all. I have loved working with you. I have loved these years together. And I deeply apologize for everything I did and didn't do that brought us to this awful day."

THE END OF THE MANHATTAN PROJECT was a death for me. I gave up directing. Or it gave up me. I didn't return for another twelve long years. I said "fuck you" to it all. I had blown my way out of the regional theater. I had blown my way out of the Broadway theater. I had had success after success, internationally and at home, but something was wrong. There was something I was still unable to express, but I couldn't imagine how or where to do that. I had to change, whatever the cost. But in order to change, I had to destroy everything I'd built. I had to burn down my *career* to go where my *vocation* was leading.

Once again, it might have been a good time to turn more of my attention to family. Instead, as I too often did then, I worried about myself and headed, literally and figuratively, into the wilderness.

16

MY MOTHER, LYDIA, didn't know anything about mothering and didn't have a talent for it. She joked about it, as she did about much that was painful for her. "Having babies makes your breasts so awwwglee," she'd complain in her Russian accent. Of course, in her generation, you had children, maternal instinct or not. You didn't question the need. My mother's war with her firstborn (me) allegedly began when I was still in the womb. She claimed I tortured her for three days by refusing to "come out."

THE BOURGEOIS MOTHER I grew up with had little left of the Russian bohemian she had been. She was a lady who lunched. On her way to a fashionable Manhattan watering hole one afternoon, her fine red cape got caught in the taxi door as she exited. The taxi dragged her half a block before pedestrians flagged it down. Mother was severely bruised, but she wouldn't miss her appointment with the ladies. She went to the hospital *after* lunch.

What else do I know about her? She loved to gamble—gin rummy and poker for high stakes. After World War II, my parents would visit friends in the Netherlands, Baron and Baroness van Zuylen, he a distinguished, monocle-wearing playboy, she a mannish Egyptian, whose father had been jailed as a horse thief. The couple would invite my parents to their ugly, rambling castle along with nouveau-riche jet-setters from all over Europe. The gambling would begin after lunch and break just before dinner. Guests would retire and dress formally to dine at a long, candlelit banquet table. Once, for the fun of it, the guests dressed the liveried servants in their own fancy clothes, while they dressed in the livery of the servants. The guests served the servers. What grotesque fun! (This would inspire a production I did of Anouilh's *Poor Bitos*. Any wonder why I went into the theater?) After dinner they gambled till dawn. The baroness was so obsessed with gambling that when the king of Spain's cousin visited, she introduced him as the cousin of the king of Spades.

When it came to ruling-class dress-up parties, my mother could be every bit as dramatic as the baroness. For instance, she often wore a turban, maybe to make her look taller. Because she was superstitious—broken-mirror, no-shoes-on-the-bed superstitious—she wouldn't allow thirteen at the table. When she threw a Hollywood luncheon and realized she was about to seat the unlucky number, she dressed an African American grounds-keeper in her turban and palmed him off to her guests as an Indian maharaja.

So my theatrical mother loved to gamble and she loved tough men. Errol Flynn, an alcoholic, bisexual womanizer (and probable Nazi spy), as I've mentioned, was one. Another was the charming tough who lived down the block in Beverly Hills, Bugsy Siegel, a thug who had built the grand Pink Flamingo casino in Las Vegas. The same Bugsy who was murdered gangland-style by the Mafia shortly after my mother had returned home from his all-night poker game.

A FOUR-YEAR-OLD BOY and his young mother are riding a train from France to Switzerland. The train passes through Germany. At the border, a member of the Gestapo comes into the car to inspect their passports. The little boy notices that his young mother has gone white as a sheet. It is 1938. The boy will never forget.

ONE MOTHER'S DAY, I was visiting the ashram of my guru, Gurumayi. They like to celebrate everything on the ashram, and so we were celebrating our mothers. The guru urged us to love the women who brought us into the world. Seeing our sour responses, she suddenly burst into laughter. "You know, if you feel your mother didn't love you, forget it. And forgive. It had nothing to do with you. Some people don't like dogs. Some don't like cats. And some just don't like children."

MY MOTHER'S FATHER was a distinguished lawyer. One uncle, a renowned doctor, got called to the Kremlin the night Stalin's wife died, killed either by Stalin himself or, less likely, by her own hand. (This uncle never returned from his house call, but in those days you didn't ask questions.) My mother and her parents lived in a spacious house, even during early Communist times.

She adored her father. In one awful childhood story, my mother described returning from school and being told by a servant that her father had died. Grief-stricken, she ran up the marble steps to his bedroom. Her father's body was laid out on the bed, covered with flowers. She went to him, distraught. Perhaps she kissed him on the forehead. Then he jumped up: "Surprise! Surprise! I'm alive." I don't know how frequently he played this game or how much she believed it after that first time, but he repeated it more than once.

WHEN I WAS IN MY SIXTIES, I got it into my head to visit my family's summer home in East Hampton; I hadn't been there in years. The house had strong echoes of the Eugene O'Neill family home in *Long Day's Journey into Night*, but in place of O'Neill's mother, strung out on morphine, we had my father, threatening to kill himself. I remember our fear, permeating the summerhouse all through my childhood. I decided to visit and explain to the owners that my family had once lived there. I would ask to take a peek around. When I arrived, however, the circular driveway was carless and the door was unlocked, so I went in and made myself at home.

Wandering around the house I realized that I was now older than either of my parents had been when we lived there. She had been in her early forties, he in his early fifties. He was in the black depths of an awful depression. She, not even knowing what was wrong with him, was trying to help. There was no medication then for manic depression.

I remembered how hard I'd worked to cheer him up, to help

him see the world in a better light. I thought of a passage from *Endgame*, the Samuel Beckett play I directed four times over forty years: "I once knew a madman . . . I'd take him by the hand and drag him to the window. Look! There! All that rising corn! . . . The sails of the herring fleet! . . . He'd snatch away his hand . . . Appalled. All he had seen was ashes."

My father had seen ashes, again and again. If it was hard for me, how must it have been for my mother? My mother was, then, younger than my daughter is now. My father lived in pain and confusion. Alone in the house on that day, I was overcome with compassion for these two young people, my parents. They were troubled and terrified. They had been mediocre parents or worse, but they had done their best under difficult, even horrific circumstances. I was filled with compassion and forgiveness. She had brought me into the world, hard as it was for her. And he had saved me from the Nazis.

A JUNGIAN ANALYST ONCE URGED, after listening to me diss my parents: "Let it drop once and for all. They were not your parents. They were merely the spaceship that brought you to earth. If you met them for the first time at a cocktail party, how long would you talk to them before heading to the bar for another drink?"

ALTHOUGH MY MOTHER and I never stopped fighting, there was one day in our life together when things were different. We were in Monte Carlo, and she suggested we take a walk. I think she knew that death was close. "You know about these things," she said. "Do you believe in an afterlife?"

I admitted that I did, that everything in nature seems to live on. After all the trouble of this life, all the seeking, all the questioning, I didn't believe that everything could halt in the middle of a sentence. She found this comforting.

We walked and we talked, as we never had before, our bodies almost touching, our conversation deeply personal. She was suddenly so sweet—unmasked, tender, and vulnerable. We had a lovely breakfast together and talked more. She told me about a dream she had had the previous night, something about Christmas, a white sepulcher, and a slab of marble. What did I think it meant?

We both knew it was a dream about death. For Christmas, she gave me the Ibsen biography and inscribed the dream inside. She added, "I hope I'll be here next Christmas."

MY MOTHER, who smoked two packs of cigarettes a day, died after a prolonged battle with lung cancer. As she was dying, they made the mistake of resuscitating her, so she suffered two more months of awful pain and rage. Her final words to me: "The whole thing was a mistake. I shouldn't have married him. I shouldn't have had children. If I get through this alive, I'll dump you all. Get me some caviar."

When I returned with the caviar, she was gone.

17

EVERYTHING, IT SEEMED, had died: our company, my career, and my mother. She would never become the person she might have been. If you had asked me, I would have admitted to feeling no love for her, and yet I entered a period of extreme grief. It was grief for a love she could now never give me. My desire to make art—to be the artist I might have been—felt like it had died with her. I played out my father's worst nightmare: a depressed life without work, the life of a bum. During my father's bipolar depressions, sobbing, he would say to me: "I have no work, I have no work, I'm a bum." His phrase became my mantra.

The times, too, fell into a gray, mournful anticlimax, following Nixon's resignation and the end of the Vietnam War. The energy and anger that had brought my generation into the streets drained away. Our theaters had reflected the bodily exuberance of the times—dancing in the streets of the East Village and Haight-Ashbury, whirling in a purple haze at Woodstock, antiwar mediators trying to levitate the Pentagon. The mammoth antiwar marches on Washington were maybe the greatest theatrical events of all. I remember marching myself and seeing the rooftops lined with national guardsmen, armed to the teeth, standing elbow to elbow. I thought, *This is the end, the end of the United States. No, not yet. Not yet.*

The end of all that physicality came not with a bang, but with a fizzle. We were left with the numb malaise of life under Gerald Ford and Jimmy Carter, a far cry from the world we'd fought and protested for, a recession-era ghost of what we'd imagined. The Reagan eighties approached, and with them all the worst impulses of selfish, inhumane, wealth-worshipping capitalism. We had been people of action—collective action. That, too, had come to an end.

THE REVOLUTIONARY THEATER of the 1960s and '70s, a period when groups of like-minded people made theater together, had likewise reached a cul-de-sac. The Manhattan Project had been only one of a constellation of experimental ensembles to form in the sixties, following the example of Julian Beck and Judith Malina's revolutionary Living Theatre. The Living Theatre had started by doing poetic, avant-garde plays by the likes of Gertrude Stein, Kenneth Rexroth, and William Carlos Williams Off Broadway in the forties and fifties, part of a community that included friends of Malina and Beck like John Cage, the composer, and the choreographer Merce Cunningham. In the sixties Malina and Beck took to the streets in America and across the globe, with anarchic spectacles calling for the overthrow of what they called the "Capitalist-Bureaucratic-Military-Authoritarian Police Complex." The pure artistic experiments of Joseph Chaikin and the Open Theater, the fabulous no-holds-barred theatricality of Charles Ludlam and the Ridiculous Theatrical Company, the heady philosophical total-theater brew of Richard Foreman's Ontological-Hysteric Theater, as well as my own Manhattan Project—we followed after the Becks, as they were known, growing up (and in some cases blowing up) side by side. We saw each other's work, stopped each other for long intimate conversations on Village streets, and knew we were part of something world- or, at least, theater-changing. When I took my mother to Ludlam's *Bluebeard*, she nearly died with laughter at the sight of Ludlam flying through the air and seemingly into the actress Lola Pashalinski's vagina. Several of these companies, along with Richard Schechner's Performance Group and Meredith Monk's House, were part of a coalition Chiquita formed with Schechner in 1973 to get grants and arrange international touring: A Bunch of Experimental Theaters. By 1977, the Bunch, also, dispersed.

MY BUM DAYS ticked endlessly by, empty days, empty months. I was frightened that my work in the theater seemed to be over for good. I once read a story about a well-to-do boy who was so lonely that he would wander around his apartment, touching the furniture to reassure himself that he was still alive. That was me.

Sometimes late at night I would sit in my study with the tape machine and let the voice of Vsevolod Meyerhold, that great dead martyr of Soviet theater, come through me. I became a strange, mad Meyerhold medium. Was I was getting closer and closer to some kind of mental collapse? I consoled myself recalling that Eleonora Duse, probably the greatest actress of all time, had given up the theater to tend her own literal garden. She stayed away for twelve years before returning. She had been transformed by that time away, I knew, and she'd returned to the stage even more luminous and transcendent. Was I searching for that, too? Still, her example was cold comfort during those long, painful years.

Then my friend Jerzy Grotowski, knowing what I was experiencing, invited me to the "Theater of Nations" gathering in Poland. There I came in contact with his "paratheatrical" work, unscripted encounters that didn't make a distinction between the performers and spectators—everyone was part of the theatrical event.

My own paratheatrical experiences took place in a Polish forest with a group of forty Polish rebels and hippies Jerzy had gathered for me, a huge, magical forest with trees so large that four or five people holding hands still couldn't wrap their arms around them. We camped together by the ruins of a little castle. We began "work" at sunset and improvised, sometimes just moving among the trees, forming and reforming as groups of all sizes, playing out small scenes, sometimes unwitnessed, often communicating only with our bodies and sound—no words. As the sun rose again in the morning we would begin to sing and dance. We'd eat together in the late morning—bread and jam, cheese and tea—and by then the food tasted better than anything you can imagine. Then we'd sleep, from noon, maybe, to sunset, before starting again. I was unmoored from anything I knew.

I DON'T KNOW what Chiquita and the children thought of it all (and I still don't like to think about that). I was gone, and I must have been, in a sense, lost to them, as I was lost to myself. I thought about my marriage almost nonstop, though. Chiquita and I were growing old together, but we weren't together. There was an enormous, sad gulf between us. I didn't understand it.

AFTER POLAND, I traveled to the Tunisian Sahara with two actors and a Japanese Buddhist priest named Kozan. I had the idea that we would find a way to adapt *The Little Prince*, Antoine de Saint-Exupéry's story of being plane-wrecked in the desert. We rode camels under an enormous sky full of brilliant stars. We rode and rode, but all I could think about was my marriage. I believed that this priest, Kozan, who would later drive our household into chaos, might be the teacher I was looking for. I would listen to his beautiful bass voice coming from across the sand, and I would follow it. We would meditate together, and then I would meditate alone, but all I would see was Chiquita's face, growing old, her hair going gray as in a time-lapse film. The desert was desolate. The nights were cold. I was searching but not finding.

One night, desperate, we just started to eat sand. We just ate sand and threw up. Then we gave up the project and went home. I was, and would continue to be, in despair.

A GROUP OF STRANGERS gathered at Richard Avedon's property on Long Island—wild, Heathcliff country at that time. It was All Souls' Eve. Three people dressed in sheets led us to the ruined basement of a burned-down house and asked us to compose our last will and testament. As midnight on Halloween turned, these sheeted people came for me and ran me through the fields. Then they undressed me, took my valuables, sponged me down, and took photographs of me naked. They ran me again through the woods and threw me down in a pile of sheets with other naked bodies, huddled together, trying to keep warm.

Then, after maybe an hour, they blindfolded us, one at a time, and took us away. When it was my turn, I was blindfolded and laid out on some kind of stretcher and carted slowly through the woods.

I felt myself being lowered into a grave. They had dug several such graves, each six or eight feet deep. They piled wood on me, stuffed my valuables in my hands, and covered me head to toe with canvas, before shoveling dirt over me—burying me alive. This is completely true and even now completely terrifying.

18

WHEN I TOLD MY FRIEND the poet Jean Valentine that I had begun keeping a diary she said to me, "Only put down the facts, not the feeling. If you put down the feelings, you will forget the facts. If you put down the facts, you will remember the feelings." This diary and the many diaries that followed contained these stories, the ones that became the basis for *My Dinner with André*.

And its first audience? Convicts in a halfway house. I gave a workshop there in storytelling. These men were the only people I knew who not only believed my stories, but had stories as strange as my own. One convict told me that, sitting on his windowsill and looking into an empty courtyard, he saw his brother rush across the courtyard, a policeman behind, and get shot. He had imagined it happening, seen it: the cop shooting his brother in the back. The next day the thing he had pictured sitting there actually happened. To these men, my kind of stories, my experiences, were not weird, not nuts. They all had experienced things like this.

TIMES WERE DESPERATE and so I turned to desperate measures. I wanted to get my stories out in any way I could, but my options were limited. So one day I called my friend Wally Shawn's father, William Shawn, at *The New Yorker*, and said to him: "Mr. Shawn, you keep printing these profiles of great artists. What do you think of doing a profile of a failure?" He liked the idea.

He assigned a *New Yorker* writer, Calvin Tomkins, to me. Tomkins never left my side. And then, after some months, he wandered off to do a profile of a successful artist. I was getting nowhere again. More diaries, more writing from the unconscious, more talks with Meyerhold. I could tell that my parents thought my life a huge disappointment. What had happened to that successful theater director who had created *Alice*? Where had he gone? A flash in the pan. I contemplated training to become a psychoanalyst.

19

I AM SITTING on the Truro beach and the sun has just set. In the afterglow of that sunset I think I see every color that has ever been put on a canvas. A lone fisherman trolls for stripers. His clothes look as if they have been in his family for generations. And down by the gentle surf a father plays with his two children. It is getting colder and the youngest of the boys, around five, is beginning to turn a bit blue. They have clearly been out here for many hours, building castles in the sand. Ornate castles with towers and turrets and moats filled with seawater. They are still having a grand time, the dad most of all. They run into the waves to fill their pink pails with water. And they laugh. And talk. I feel shame knowing my own kids didn't have a dad like that. And sadness that I didn't have that kind of dad.

It's growing dark. The dad and his two kids pick up their shovels, pails, and towels, as the tide sweeps away the castles they built so lovingly.

ON HIS FIRST DATE with the woman who would become his wife, Matisse warned her not to get her hopes up; he would never put love before his art. I remember a young actress in group therapy. In one session she said something like, "I can never get out of myself. I am always looking at myself. I sit on the toilet and wonder, 'What do I look like on the toilet?' I take a shit and wonder, 'Do I look differently when I'm shitting from when I'm not shitting?' I hate. I hate it!"

I WAS, IN MANY WAYS, "there but not there" with my children, Nicholas and Marina. I was twenty-six when I became a father. I so wanted to be different to them from the way my father was to me. But I had had no lessons, no good examples. The very word "father" had confusing and unpleasant associations. My own father may have been nuts—he was nuts—but what about me, the André who let himself be buried alive in Montauk?

IN WALLACE SHAWN'S PLAY *The Designated Mourner*, the central character reflects, "When I was growing up, there was an uncle of mine who always used to tell me, 'Look, we are rats. All of our family have always been rats, and you, too, will be a rat, my boy. Remember that, and you won't go wrong, because it's really all quite simple: The skills rats possess don't work under water, so avoid getting wet. Don't abandon the sinking ship unless another boat's nearby to board. And, for God's sake, don't be ashamed of being a rat. Rats aren't bad, they're not mean or cruel, they're simply doing what they can to survive.'"

YOU HAVE TO MAKE the right decision to survive. Each decision my father made about where to go next was calculated and calculated and calculated. He calculated in order to stay ahead of the horrific march of events in Europe. Did he cut deals to get out? Was he a calculating and lucky survivor, a rat, or both?

The truth is: I believe that my father, a Jewish businessman, collaborated with the Nazis. I'll never know for sure. The evidence is circumstantial, but there's so much of it. My father and his brothers owned an apartment building in Berlin until 1941. How could that be? How as Jews could they have been allowed to do that? In Paris, he received visits from Hitler's foreign minister, Joachim von Ribbentrop. Why in the world would they meet? When Father first returned to Germany after the war he met with a good friend from before, the head of the Hitler Youth for Women. One of our summer guests in Europe was the son of another of my father's friends, then on trial in Nuremberg. Our guest had been in the Hitler Youth, too. He boasted that every SS man was so virile he could fill a milk pail with his sperm. I was too young to understand what the hell he meant.

I know my father worked with the Germans, but that is certainly different than *collaborating*. He may have been a rat. I believe he was, but I can't *know*. And none of us can know what we would have done under the same circumstances.

Every summer in the fifties we visited Paris, so that my father could do business there. One memorable evening, we were dining in a nice restaurant when the headwaiter came to the table to say that someone wished to speak to my father. Father didn't come back. He had been arrested by the French secret service.

The following days were frightening. For maybe a week we couldn't locate him. My mother's friend, a prominent lawyer, flew over from Washington. The lawyer tracked Father down and got him released. In the family lore it was all a case of mistaken identity. I, of course, have long suspected it was connected to his dealings with Germany before the war.

20

IT IS SAID THAT YOU have to wait many, many lifetimes for the blessing of the teacher to appear, to experience the teacher's clear and luminous look, like a sun ray. I felt it first with Grotowski, my first true teacher in the theater. And I felt it again when I met the Rinpoche of Ladakh.

It was after the breakup of the Manhattan Project, during the feverish years that led me to the Polish forest, the Saharan desert, and the mock graveyard in Montauk. I wanted to go to Tibet, but it was impossible. Tibet had been taken over by Communist China and was closed to outsiders.

In the late 1970s the Rockefeller Foundation sent me to Dharamsala, the seat of the Dalai Lama, to work with Tibetan refugees. Historically, only Tibetan monks had chanted sacred operas and danced sacred dances, but with so many refugees in other countries setting up Tibetan centers, it was often left to the non-monk refugees from Tibet to do the chanting and dancing. Many suffered from stage fright. I was sent to Dharamsala to help them overcome their fear of performing.

One day, during a break in my stage fright workshops, a monk asked me if I would like to go to Ladakh, wherever the hell that was. *Sure*, I thought. *Why not?* So the monk and I got on a bus, which I believe was the first civilian bus up to Ladakh in the forty years it had been cordoned off by the Indian Army. They had closed the area because of its strategic location on the borders of India, Pakistan, and Tibet.

My *calling*, that tempting genie, was whispering in my ear yet again: "This way. This way."

I began a harrowing trip of three days on a rickety old bus, around hairpin turns, along cliffs thousands of feet high. My liver was in my throat. What was I, a husband and father, doing traveling God knows where, risking my life on a journey from which I might not return? This is what I meant about the sin of being an artist who puts his art before everything—and everyone—else.

After three or four days I arrived on a barren landscape 10,000 feet above sea level. Nothing there but desert. One tiny hardware store. That was it. Nothing to eat but Tibetan tea, a mixture of tea, salt, and yak butter. I found it disgusting. The monk put me up on a farm way out in the country. No one had seen a foreigner in more than forty years, so when I went down to the river in the morning to brush my teeth, the entire village would come to watch. One morning I turned a corner in the village, and a little girl fled in terror. She had probably never seen anything so monstrous.

Why in hell had I come here? I had no one to talk with

and nothing to eat. There was nothing to do. About a week later—suddenly, providentially—two women, Buddhist pilgrims, passed through this godforsaken land in a jeep. They took me to a monastery. We entered a room with very, very high ceilings and a few small vertical windows. The floor was covered with sawdust. Sitting on the floor were twenty-four monks, twelve and twelve, facing one another, chanting and playing ancient instruments.

The walls were covered with gifts that had been pressed into them by thousands of visiting pilgrims. I was stunned. I couldn't breathe. I felt as if a donkey had kicked me in the stomach. I discovered later that every time a monk fell asleep, another monk would enter to take his place. Every time a monk died, another monk would enter to take his place. These monks had been playing and chanting without stopping—without stopping—for more than four hundred years.

From there the two pilgrims drove me to Hemis Monastery, also in Ladakh. It looked like a building out of a ghost town, run-down, dilapidated, with tattered prayer flags fluttering in the wind. There was no one around until a German abbot appeared and asked us if we would like to have darshan with the Rinpoche. A man entered the room, and the two women immediately prostrated themselves on the floor.

I didn't know what to do. Should I go to the ground like them to be polite, or would that be hypocritical? I was too awkward and confused about protocol to even look at the man himself. And then I did.

Let me point out here that I was not, at that point in my life, a spiritual man. I had no interest in spiritual books. I considered myself an agnostic. I was like Saul of Tarsus, a businessman on his way to Damascus when he saw Christ. Saul's life was changed forever: He became Paul. The businessman became the apostle.

I know that what I'm about to say will, to some, seem far-fetched and unbelievable, just as I find it far-fetched that an image shot thousands of miles away can appear instantly on my television, that I can talk into a glass tablet and letters will appear on the face of the tablet. My story would not seem unbelievable to Teresa of Avila, though. Some believe in the miraculous, and others simply don't. Some stay rooted, feet on the ground, and some adventure and pursue the invisible. In *My Dinner with André*, there is an André who believes and a Wally who never will. The film needs both to exist. Probably we all do.

Anyway, I finally looked up to see the Rinpoche. There, sitting on a small raised throne, was a paunchy, elderly man with a long, long beard. I looked into his eyes. What I saw there seemed not so much eyes as planets. These planets were all light.

I began to weep, and he began to laugh. The laughter I heard sounded like magnificent bells. I began to roar with laughter. He laughed more at my laughter, and I began to weep again. I laughed and wept and wept and laughed. He spoke in a language I couldn't understand, and, at the end of whatever he was saying, he took me by the hand and led me to the window. He pointed at the desert landscape. It was early afternoon but the skies suddenly went black. Comets were streaking across the sky.

AS WE DROVE OUT of the monastery I was overtaken by a love more powerful than anything I had ever experienced. I adored him. I loved him. All I wanted to do was stay with him.

21

WALLY CALLED ME and said something like, "Listen, I know what you're going through, and when I'm your age I don't want to go through it myself. So in order for me to prevent that, what do you think of the two of us sitting together, you telling me your stories, and out of that we might create a talking heads TV show?" Not an earth-shattering idea, but okay. Sure, why not?

And so we sat in a tiny classroom in New York and talked. We recorded these talks on tape. We began each day with a story of mine. They weren't all about eating sand in the Sahara with a Buddhist monk or being buried alive. Just stories. About anything at all.

The stories would become conversation. About anything at all.

We talked and talked. It was fun. It was fun to be with Wally. It was a relief to *do* something. And it was great not to be alone. It went on this way for months. We discussed almost everything.

WALLY TOOK THE COUNTLESS HOURS of transcript and reduced it to a script. Even so, Wally had written one of the longest screenplays ever, with a role for André that would become, I believe, the longest speaking role in the history of film.

AS IF ANYONE IN THE WORLD would want to direct a movie written by and starring two unknowns, who sit at a table for hours and do nothing but talk, we set out to determine the perfect director for *My Dinner with André* (a title so mundane that I wanted to change it). Bergman would be good, we thought, if only he had a sense of humor. Richard Avedon might be interesting, if only he were a director and not a photographer. Eric Rohmer? Not profound enough. We considered nearly every movie director alive to shoot our "masterpiece." But even if someone would agree to direct this lunatic project, who in the world would want to see it, except for a handful of friends and loved ones?

ONE DAY MY FRIEND Diana Michener came over for tea. Diana, a fine photographer, told me she was shooting a series on death. I said something like: "Wanna see death? I can show you death." I put on a suit Pierre Cardin had given me when *Alice* opened at his Paris theater. I always thought it made me look like a vampire. "Oh my god," she said. "You do look like death. May I shoot you in that suit?" "Sure. Why not?"

We shot the pictures in her studio. We planned to go to dinner afterward, and Wally, also a good friend of hers, came by to pick us up. He carried our "masterpiece" under his arm. An admirer of Wally's plays, Diana asked to read the screenplay. "Sure. Why not?"

A COUPLE NIGHTS LATER I got a call from a man with an odd French accent. He claimed to be Louis Malle. He had just finished our script and sounded as if he were in tears. "If you don't want me to direct it," he said, "I would love to produce it. The only thing... I beg you ... *no flashbacks*. It must stay as it is." Was it a hoax? No, it wasn't. We not only had our director; we had one of the finest in the world.

AT THE END of our first evening together, Louis looked at me sharply. "If we do this, André," he said, "it'll be the most difficult thing you have ever done." And how right he was.

First, I had to memorize hundreds of pages of dialogue. I would learn fifteen pages and try for another two. But as I learned the new pages, three others would slip away. This went on for nine months. Sometimes, worried awake, I would get out of bed, make coffee, and go back to memorizing. I practiced everywhere—on the subway, in Colorado, where I went to lead a workshop, on a two-week holiday with Chiquita in Mexico. It spoiled her vacation. If I stopped for even a day, I would begin to forget.

THERE WAS ALSO THE ISSUE of money. We had to raise a hell of a lot of it to make this work. Everyone we approached thought we were nuts. A good friend who had invested in many of my productions over the years reprimanded me: "You know what? I'm deeply hurt. I've helped you for years, and now you're asking me to put money in something that will not only lose all its money but is silly and stupid. You should be ashamed of yourselves." I asked an old friend who headed the National Endowment for the Arts for a small grant to cover the costs of videotaping rehearsals to plan camera angles ahead of time (we would never be able to afford a long film shoot). We met at her home, and I described the project. When I finished she said, "I haven't understood a single word. I don't know what the hell you think you are doing. I've helped you in the past, but I'm certainly not going to help you with this bullshit."

Louis had always raised money through the usual movie channels, which were closed to us with a small, strange project like this. He kindly joined Wally and me when we made our pitch to the wealthy. For him—for all of us—it was a humiliating experience.

LOUIS TAUGHT ME how to act for film. He gave me one direction: Speak faster. Was he demanding that because I was so boring? No, I was used to theater acting, he told me, and this had to be film acting. (This was the same direction John Huston gave to his father, Walter Huston, also a theater actor, in their film *The Treasure of the Sierra Madre*, and it won Walter an Oscar.) The role was already there—in my eyes—Louis explained. I'd done so much rehearsing, I didn't have to "act" or "perform." The camera sees everything. Talking fast would take my mind off acting. It would help me create "André," a character who is driven, obsessed, and narcissistic, who delights in the sound of his own voice.

Even with this direction, though, I didn't yet have a character.

The film's André was modeled on this André (me). He said things André said, more or less. But he was not real-life André. A character who looks and sounds like André but isn't really André? Which parts of me were me? Which were right for the role? Who the hell was I anyway? We are all many faceted. I have been thrown out of four gyms in my life for horsing around; would anyone know *that* André? I couldn't answer the central, spiritual question: Who am I? This part of the work—finding the man who was and wasn't André, and in the process finding myself—was the hardest of all.

Then one day out of nowhere, after months of rehearsing, I had it. I found four *voices*: André the flighty, off-the-wall rich kid; André the guru (à la Peter Brook); André the spiritual used-car salesman; and the sincere André (who appears briefly at the end of the film). I had my André, the character Wally had based on me and on my life and stories.

But we still had one problem: We still hadn't raised any money. "You know, boys, I love this project, but I can't spend the rest of my life on it," Louis said.

The theater critic John Lahr suggested we do *My Dinner with André* as a staged reading at London's Royal Court Theatre. Nothing to lose. We rehearsed once. Our set: a table and two chairs. When I walked onstage to hug Wally, I was horrified to see, in this small, small theater, an audience full of British theater legends. They hadn't come to see Wally and me—no one knew us then. They came because it was their custom to attend openings at the Court. I wanted to go home. I still hadn't memorized all my lines, so I had someone in the front row "on book." My knees were actually knocking. I didn't know knees really did that outside of comic books.

· · ·

WE BEGAN. Total silence from the audience. The silence lasted maybe twenty minutes. What the hell do these unknown Yanks think they are doing? What is this? What the hell is an experimental beehive in a Polish forest? We were dying up there.

Finally—suddenly—a few, scattered laughs. Then more. And more. And more. The audience roared with laughter. We were a hit, a strange, unique sensation.

Michael White, the legendary producer of *The Rocky Horror Picture Show* and *Monty Python and the Holy Grail*, congratulated us backstage. He wanted to produce our movie. It was all happening; we couldn't believe it. It was coming together. But where would we shoot it? A New York union crew would be way out of our budget. And we couldn't afford to shut down a New York City restaurant for twelve days. Indeed, in those days, even with White's backing, we had very little money.

BUT CERTAIN PROJECTS, I've learned, have a life of their own. Out of nowhere, the *Atlantic City* assistant costume designer mentioned to Louis that his father had recently purchased a long-abandoned grand hotel in the Old South—Richmond, Virginia. The lobby boasted empty alligator pools and a majestic staircase that had inspired the one Rhett Butler carried Scarlett O'Hara up in *Gone With the Wind*: "Frankly, my dear, I don't give a damn."

We had a set.

WE DID HAVE ONE PROBLEM, though. It was cold, very cold. The only way to heat the set was to heat the entire hotel, and we had no budget for that. Thus, we began filming as if we were doing a documentary in Antarctica. The crew wore ski clothes, earmuffs, thick gloves. Between takes they brought in heat lamps. Next shot, we would freeze again. If you know *My Dinner with André*, you'll get the irony: Under the table, I had an electric blanket draped over my knees. I wore long johns under my elegant outfit. Downed a shot of brandy between some takes. Louis had been right. Nothing, nothing about this movie was easy.

ANOTHER OBSTACLE: finding the right waiter. A critical role, because he's really the only other actor in the movie, punctuating the scenes between Wally and André. We saw many actors. Some were elderly and, for good reason, unknown. Some were too well known to appear with the two of us unknowns. As shooting got closer, I called Richard Avedon, who never forgot a face. I described what we were looking for. Dick said: "I used to know a guy who would be perfect. If he's still alive." The man he told me about wasn't an actor. He worked as a technical director for film, somewhere in the bowels of the Museum of Modern Art. Used to be a successful film distributor in Austria, but fled the Nazis.

He was still alive. We brought him down to Richmond. A day into shooting, though, Louis wanted to fire him. He had no idea how to serve a table. Wally and I stayed up all night teaching him. It worked. Jean Lenauer was wonderful in the role. After the film came out, Jean, despite his years and total inexperience as an actor, became a minor celebrity, speaking at universities, surrounded by admiring young women.

OUR TAKES WERE TWELVE MINUTES LONG. We were shooting film, not video, so no taping over our mistakes. In many movies, takes last about three minutes, and even within those short, three-minute takes actors often flub their lines. I could do twelve without missing a word. The sound technicians couldn't believe it.

YEARS LATER WALLY and I were walking down the street when a fan ran up to Wally. "My god!" he exclaimed. "*My Dinner with André* is my favorite film of all time, and you"—meaning Wally—"were *great*! So great." He went on and on about how great Wally was without ever looking at me. Finally, Wally pointed at me and said, "I guess you know my friend?" He didn't. "I was the other guy," I admitted. He went back to praising Wally. In time he walked away. Then he rushed back. "I'm so sorry," he said to me. "You were the waiter!! You were great." And off he went.

THE MOVIE FIRST SCREENED for an audience at the Telluride Film Festival. Telluride takes place every Labor Day weekend in that lovely western town under a range of high mountains. The sky is brilliantly blue, and, at 9,000 feet, it's hard to breathe. *My Dinner with André* screened at an old opera house. Same response as at the Royal Court in London. Twenty minutes of complete, bewildered silence. Wally and I were excruciatingly nervous. Then laughs. Then roars of laughter. The standing ovation seemed to last forever—I believe it went on for fourteen minutes. The crowd carried us down Main Street in a "victory" march.

The New York Film Festival was next. My teenage son, Nick, hired a limo to drive the six blocks to the opening. He gave me a white silk scarf, the kind Ronald Colman, the movie idol, would have worn. Again, a terrific response.

Until the reviews came out. They were, mostly, awful. Given

the film's later success, few recall how bad those first reviews were. As I remember it, *The New York Times* said it was a sweet, Winnie-the-Pooh-style fable, if you like that sort of thing. *Time* described it as a failed NYU Film School project with amateur actors, no script, and no director. I seldom read reviews and never remember them. But I read this set. They were bad enough—which was a shock—that we anticipated the future for *My Dinner with André* as a rare screening in an occasional Louis Malle retrospective.

We had opened in four theaters, in New York, Boston, Los Angeles, and San Francisco. We had no advertising budget. Even if we had, it would have done no good. We heard reports of Saturday audiences of eight. We had a giant flop on our hands, a film almost no one wanted to see. Up the block was one of the biggest, pre-AIDS gay hits ever, *Taxi Zum Klo* (*Taxi to the Toilet*). Gay men poured in from all over New England to see it. Lines down the block. I was so desperate, I would stand in line and tell the guys around me that if they couldn't get tickets to this movie, there was another great movie a few blocks away that was also about two men . . .

THEN OUR LUCK TURNED. Gene Siskel and Roger Ebert, who had seen the film at Telluride, dedicated an entire episode of their TV show, *At the Movies*, to singing our praises. A few weeks later they named *My Dinner with André*, along with *Reds*, as the best films of the year. Overnight, theaters around the country wanted *My Dinner with André*. The film became a huge hit and never stopped attracting viewers. I think it played in New York, L.A., and Boston for something like two years. Since then, generation after generation has seen it, including tens of millions of hits on YouTube.

DESPITE OUR "HIT," I couldn't find my way back to directing. I made my living playing small roles in a dozen blockbuster movies: *Demolition Man* with Sylvester Stallone and Wesley Snipes, *The Mosquito Coast* with Harrison Ford, *Protocol* with Goldie Hawn. I'm only proud of playing John the Baptist in Martin Scorsese's *The Last Temptation of Christ*. I still act in films and on television. But now, in my later years, I get offered nothing but bit parts as Alzheimer's patients and ancient child molesters.

PEOPLE OFTEN ASK US if we will ever make a sequel to *My Dinner with André*. We had an idea for a follow-up, but we'll never film it. How could we without Louis? The sequel would feature me at ninety, if I live that long, and Wally at eighty. In place of a dinner table and an elegant Manhattan restaurant, picture two old men in rocking chairs on the veranda of an Adirondacks hotel. They talk about only one thing, the one subject never mentioned in *My Dinner with André*: sex.

22

GRISHA, MY FATHER, was devastated that I became an artist. He was well into his eighties when *My Dinner with André* came out, and we had one of our awful fights. After the fight my wife, Chiquita, went to his place, to make sure he was all right. "I don't know what's wrong with André," he said. "Why does he always have to fight with me?" Chiquita said to him, "I think sometimes André feels you don't respect him." "Don't respect him? Don't respect him? Of course I respect him. He could've been a great lawyer!" From this distance it reads like an old Jewish joke.

To give him credit, though, he did remove from the wall a Chagall painting he had bought in Paris in the thirties and replace it with a poster of *My Dinner with André*. (I learned after his death that the painting was a fake.) He had invested $500 in the film and was delighted when it actually made money. But he was a businessman through and through. I'll never forget the day he actually made the investment in the film. After he had handed the $500 check to the producer, and as we walked out of the building together, he had said to me: "I will never forgive you for this."

ONE TIME WE WERE having lunch together, my father and I. When we were alone, he would always order bratwurst and sauerkraut, saying to me under his breath, "Don't tell your mother." At this particular meal, I asked him a question I had never thought to ask. I had no idea who my father's grandfather was, knew nothing about him. So I asked.

A big, loving smile lit up his face. He said, "Oh, your great-grandfather Haim. I loved him. He was a lovely man." "What did Haim do?" I asked. With great pride my father replied, "Oh, Haim did nothing. Nothing. He was a *learner*."

I pointed to myself and said, "That's what I am—a learner." For a moment I think he understood.

MY FATHER BORE an uncanny resemblance to Napoleon, especially the way he stood—chin thrust upward and chest thrust out. He grew up in a Lithuanian shtetl and remembered his own father as a stern, cruel man, an Orthodox Jew and small-town businessman. If my father did anything to displease him, he would have to stand at attention—a small boy—all night, beside his sleeping father.

My father had an amazing instinct for survival. He had the

ability to see the shape of things to come. Just before he died, he told me that if he were young, he would leave the United States. Why? I asked. "Because both parties in America have become so corrupt, it can only lead to fascism. Do you know," I remember my father asking, "the only difference of opinion that Hitler and Mussolini ever had?" I had no idea. "Hitler had wanted to call their form of government 'fascism,' while Mussolini wanted to call it 'corporate totalitarianism.'"

As I read the news each day, I hear his warnings about the coming of fascism to America. What would he make of the en-trenched power of an ever-smaller wealthy class, a corrupt real estate tycoon as president, attacks on the press, and the populist raging of anti-Semites? Would he find any comfort in being right?

THOUGH HE WAS A SHTETL JEW, my father fashioned himself like a WASP gentleman golfer. Before he died in 1984, I'd been cast in an Off Broadway production of A. R. Gurney's *The Middle Ages*. I was playing a WASP patriarch and, researching the role, I studied pictures of wealthy men on the golf course and in the clubhouse. I came across a picture of my father in Hollywood in the forties. I thought he would enjoy seeing it. When I showed it to him, though, he was annoyed: "Why are you digging around in this old stuff? It's over with, finished. I can hardly remember it."

I explained that this was research and described the way I carefully built a role. I spoke without any condescension, not to the uncultivated businessman I considered him to be, but as if to a fellow artist. Something shifted. "We are alike, you and I," he said. "You build a role the way I build a building." Then, in a leap, he added, "I hated it when you would march to Washington to protest the war. But it doesn't matter what side we are on. What matters is that we are both men of principle. And that we stand by our principles."

I was very moved. He was dying at age eighty-four, the age I am now. At last, when it was almost too late, we were talking.

I HAD SEEN in an antiques store a 1920s Art Deco pocket watch. I asked him if he might give it to me as an opening night gift. "But you already have a watch," he said.

"Yes, but I could inscribe something on the back from you."

He thought a moment and, with an eloquence unusual for a man who spoke six languages and none of them well, said: "Write on it, *What a pity we let the time go by.*"

"But that's so sad."

"No, it's the truth. And the truth is never sad or happy. It's just the truth."

It was our last talk.

I learned how to say the mourner's Kaddish from an Israeli friend, and I said it over my father's grave. I am grateful to my father. Very. I have never missed him, though. Not for a moment. And that is sad, truly sad. But it's the truth.

23

CHIQUITA, IN 1989, was diagnosed with breast cancer. She was only fifty-three years old. The news hit us like a truck, barreling around a corner in the middle of the night. Cancer was still taboo then, a matter of shame. The diagnosis felt like a death sentence.

She didn't want to talk about it. She wanted to go on as if nothing out of the ordinary was happening, so she insisted that we continue working as before. I was only too happy to play along and bury my fears that she would die. There would come a time, however, when we could no longer avoid it.

. . .

AROUND THAT SAME TIME I got an offer from Shakespeare & Company, a theater company in the Berkshires, to play Prospero in *The Tempest*. My daughter, Marina, had been cast as Prospero's daughter, Miranda. I didn't like this theater company much, and I didn't trust them. I thought they were capitalizing on my new celebrity from *My Dinner with André* and using Marina to get to me. My instinct told me not to do it.

I consulted the I Ching. I threw the coins and couldn't believe what came up. I received *The Creative*. This is the I Ching equivalent of hitting the jackpot at Las Vegas. This is the I Ching telling you that your choice will bring propitious creativity and open new paths for your work. I could not believe this prediction could come true at Shakespeare & Company, but the I Ching said to do it, so I decided to take the chance.

Chiquita wanted to rest up in New York during the rehearsals, but she insisted I go. In retrospect, I believe she wanted to know that I would take good care of our daughter if she couldn't be here to do so. Playing my daughter's father onstage was one way to take care.

The rehearsals were conventional, boring and uneventful, every bit as bad as I'd feared they would be. I felt like tearing up the I Ching and throwing it in the garbage. This was my return to theater after the years in that personal wilderness that led to *My Dinner with André*. I was angry about Chiquita's illness, so I connected to Shakespeare's Prospero as a man who, having lost a wife, is on the verge of madness. Everything that happens around him, in my interpretation, he imagines. Marina hated the work so much that she'd started a project on her own with a friend, rehearsing a scene between Yelena and Sonya from Anton Chekhov's *Uncle Vanya*. She asked me to direct them.

Uncle Vanya takes place on a country estate, and nearly every character in it is dissatisfied with his or her own life and wants something they don't or can't have. This is particularly true of Vanya himself, an educated man wasting his life and talent, living with his niece and caretaking his dead sister's farm.

The moment I reread the play I thought of Wally. He would be a perfect Vanya!

CHIQUITA'S CANCER HAD METASTASIZED. I quit *The Tempest* and rushed back to the city.

For a time, our lives centered on Chiquita's illness and treatment. When a lumpectomy showed improvement and she began radiation therapy, she encouraged me, as she always did, to go back to work.

I turned my attention to *Uncle Vanya*.

VANYA WOULD BE my return to directing after twelve years away. I asked Wally to play Vanya, and he turned me down. He was not a serious actor, he said. (Our work together on great tragic roles over the next twenty-five years would prove him wrong.) I kept thinking about the angry anchorman Howard Beale in Sidney Lumet's *Network*, telling his listeners to go out on their fire escapes and shout, "I'm mad as hell, and I'm not going to take it anymore!" That was my image for Wally as Vanya. I asked him again, and he turned me down again. He turned me down four times. Finally, I said: "What if we never perform it? What if we do it simply as a workshop, to investigate the play and the role?" "Oh, if we do it that way, I would love to," he agreed.

. . .

ONE DAY MY DEAR FRIEND George Gaynes called to tell me that his thirty-one-year-old son, Matthew, a champion kayaker, had been killed in a freak traffic accident in northern India. He had been traveling to Nepal to film a kayaking special for ESPN. Even though he was sitting relatively safely in the rear of a bus, Matthew, who had just gotten married, had been instantly killed. No one else on the bus died. Matthew's memorial service in Santa Barbara was truly heartbreaking. "Director," though, is just a kinder word for "vampire," and when I looked at George, grieving his son, I could not help thinking he would be a wonderful Serebryakov in *Vanya*. Of course, I never would have asked him then, but four months later I did. He would simply not be up to performing, he said, given the grief that he was feeling. We would not perform, I promised. We would simply experiment and rehearse. We would play. In that case, he said, "I'll do it."

MY FRIEND JACK DOULIN was at the very start of a career as an important New York casting director. He told me about an actress named Julianne Moore. I'd never heard of her. I went to see Julianne in a play at the Public Theater, and found her performance very powerful. There had been an especially terrific, even frightening moment in the production when she sat totally silent, just reading a newspaper. We had dinner afterward. "What were you doing at that moment, I asked her?" "Oh, nothing," she replied. "I was counting from one to twelve." Every actor, in my experience, works in a mysterious and unique way.

STRASBERG TOLD A STORY about a play in 1920s Berlin so popular that in its second season there were two separate productions running at the same time, starring two legendary actors. Toward the end of the play there was what Stanislavski called a "star moment." The central character, determined to kill himself, puts a revolver to his head and closes his eyes. He is about to pull the trigger when a shudder goes through his body. He cannot do it. He drops the gun.

This moment was much talked about. At a press conference featuring the two actors, they were asked what they were "working on" to create such a real and terrifying effect. One said that, as he put the gun to his head, he imagined standing at his living room window and watching his five-year-old daughter run into the road and get killed by a speeding car. He shuddered with horror. The second actor imagined getting into his morning shower, turning on the water and being shocked by the ice-cold spray. He, too, closed his eyes and shuddered. Strasberg was using this story to illustrate his belief that great acting cannot be taught, that each actor has his or her own way of working. Acting is a mysterious art, and directors should approach every actor as a separate, inscrutable being.

JULIANNE MOORE HAD LITTLE INTEREST in my *Vanya* project, because she had become disappointed in the theater itself. The scripts were awful, the directors uninspiring. I believe she was even considering doing something else with her life. "So why don't you do this project? Why don't you make it a celebration of the end of your life in the theater? We'll never perform it!" "Great!" she said.

JACK DOULIN ALSO TOLD ME about the superb eighty-year-old Ruth Nelson. Ruth was one of the original members of the seminal Group Theatre, started by Strasberg, Harold Clurman, and Cheryl Crawford in the 1930s. After the Group disbanded in '39, she had been headed toward a major Broadway career when Elia Kazan cast her as Linda Loman in Arthur Miller's *Death of a Salesman*. Kazan, who had been a stage manager and undistinguished actor with the Group before becoming probably the most renowned stage and film director of the mid-twentieth century, had given names at the Joseph McCarthy–led House Un-American Activities Committee hearing, and Ruth's husband, another very fine Hollywood director, had been blacklisted because of Kazan. So she turned the role down. She turned Kazan down.

That decision meant that she never had the career she should have had, as great an actress as she was. Our work together would remind her of the best time of her life, the years with the Group. She never just called me André, always "dear, dear André." Ruth was feisty, gutsy, and determined, made of steel. In her twenties she had surgery and got hooked on the opium they gave her. To break the habit, she camped in a tent in the Nevada desert in the middle of summer, paid a young boy to bring her water every day, and sweated the opium out of her system.

Ruth was apprehensive, as she had phlebitis in her leg, which was extremely painful. I reassured her that the schedule would be easy. Plus we had no plans to ever perform the play. Because she was so sick and delicate, she had to be very careful with her energy. Careful, simple, and still. There's an old adage in the theater that you should never act with children or animals. Their simplicity makes mature actors look phony and stagey. In our case, the actors started catching Ruth's simplicity in order not to seem out of place with her. Though she never gave "direction," she directed by example.

I never audition people; I sit and talk with them. With Lynn Cohen, who would play Mama, I spent the whole interview talking about food. And then there was my old pal from Manhattan Project days, the brilliant Larry Pine, who would play Dr. Astrov.

ANOTHER ACTOR from the Manhattan Project days was Jerry Mayer, whom I hadn't seen or talked to in years. Jerry had grown up tough in orphanages after years of living with his mother, a prostitute, turning tricks in the next room. In the orphanage he taught himself fluent Russian and how to play classical violin. As an adult, Jerry smoked a lot of dope and consumed many large bottles of Coca-Cola every day. When he went into the theater he always believed that if he could be in a "hit," all his pain would go away. *Alice* was a hit, but the pain didn't go away. Jerry was quite dangerous and prone to violence. We had given him a year's paid leave with the hope he would go into therapy. He didn't go into therapy, and he never came back.

Shortly before embarking on *Vanya*, I re-met Jerry. He was playing the violin at a birthday party for my godchild. I was so touched by him and his playing that I asked him to play Waffles in *Uncle Vanya*. His performance was beautiful. It was his final role.

EVERYTHING WAS COMING TOGETHER until Chiquita decided she had had enough. She wanted to leave New York. She wanted to be somewhere people didn't know she had *cancer*. To her, cancer was a bit shameful, like a secret crime. We had previously visited friends in Santa Barbara and driven northwest from there in a rented car. We came upon this beautiful cattle country. Open farmland. Nothing but cows. Chiquita loved it. It reminded her of Argentina, happier days. And she loved nature.

I was less enthusiastic. What the hell would I do in the middle of nowhere, cut off from everyone I knew, except for Chiquita? But I didn't know what else to do but help my wife live through what might be her last years in a place that might make her happy. Maybe it would help her recover. And so what if my only friends were cows?

We sold our apartment in New York and bought a house in Santa Ynez, a town with one café and a mostly empty hotel. We couldn't talk about Chiquita's illness, and we couldn't talk about the future, whether we'd stay there if she got healthy. Soon she was busy renovating a house in the country, trying to forget the cancer.

I HATED NOT WORKING. I'd gone into the unknown and left *Vanya* behind. I sat in a little home office, reading the play over and over and over again, something I hadn't done in years. Would I ever return to directing? I was so lonely that one day, walking around the modern art museum on a trip to L.A., I went into the gift shop and filled a bag with folkloric Russian gifts—babushkas, nested dolls—and sent one to each of my actors. At the museum I also saw a tiny turn-of-the-century French seascape. Small, billowing changing tents. Women in long gowns and men in elegant suits. Children running and playing with hoops. Everyone talking and talking, and behind them a huge, gorgeous sun sets. While the people in the painting busy themselves with this and that, while they talk and talk, no one notices the sunset. The sun was setting, too, for Chiquita and me. We talked of other things. This painting became the inspiration for my work on *Uncle Vanya*. I sent postcard pictures of that seascape to the actors with their gifts and added a note: "See you soon."

24

BEFORE LONG CHIQUITA and I returned for a month's stay in the city to rehearse and see old friends. We rented a tiny apartment, the kind a young rabbinical student might have. I loved that apartment more than the spacious Upper West Side place we had inhabited for so many years.

Time, at last, to rehearse *Uncle Vanya*. My wife was ill, and I was devastated by her illness. Ruth Nelson had cancer, but didn't know it yet, on top of her painful phlebitis. George Gaynes, still mourning his son, had mysteriously disappeared, so we started without him.

Shortly after rehearsals began George phoned and asked me out to lunch. At lunch he told me that he hated his role. He saw the professor as a ruined, pompous, boring old stick. He was see-ing the role as the jealous Vanya described him, I told him, not as the character actually was. I saw Serebryakov as a charismatic lecturer, like the mythologist Joseph Campbell, whose *The Hero with a Thousand Faces* had been published in 1949 and changed the way the world thought of story and myth. Yes, the professor was like Campbell—charming, brilliant, and handsome, some-one who lectured to rows of adoring young women. I was a master of bullshit, George said. He didn't want to play the role, Joseph Campbell or old stick. I couldn't force him.

We were longtime friends. I was disappointed. When lunch was over, we put on our overcoats to face the brisk, wintry day. As we were leaving the restaurant—and I swear this was an accident, an act of God, not a setup—Julianne Moore walked through the door. I introduced George and said, "George, this is Julianne. Had you done the play, she would have been your wife." George, a born charmer with an eye for pretty women, said, "I'll do it."

THE CAST AND I SPENT the summer working on *Uncle Vanya* in a loft we had rented for around $500 a month. (How things have changed.) Rehearsals were a mix of joy and the pain of loss. Any given day George might say something like, "I don't know how I can rehearse today. I'm in so much pain." We would say, "No problem," and get coffee and Danish. We'd sit and schmooze and after an hour had passed, George might say, "Why don't we try rehearsing a little." It was the same with me. There were days—after a bad medical report about Chiquita maybe—I could hardly make it to work. Again we would sit around, joking, gossiping, and telling stories. Slowly, we'd start to rehearse.

I always try to make rehearsals joyful. This particular mixture of darkness and hope was so Chekhovian that it became the subtext of our production. But don't forget: It wasn't a production, was never meant to be. We were friends, getting together to work on *Uncle Vanya* with no goal, no reason except for the work itself. I don't remember what I paid everyone, but it wouldn't have been much.

AT THE END OF THE SUMMER, we had had such a good time we got out our calendars and found five or six days at Thanksgiving. We worked another few days at Easter and two months the next summer. Each time, when we were done, Chiquita and I headed back to California. We would work intermittently like this for a couple more years.

THE ADVANTAGE OF WORKING over so long a time is that you chip away at the stereotypes and clichés the actors—and I as a director—come in with. We think we know who these characters are, but we don't. We think we know what the play is saying, but we don't. There's too much below the surface. Over time we break through this surface to reveal what's underneath. There's always so much more there, more that emerges over time.

For example, there's a cliché about the play—and about life in general—that in a marriage between a young woman and a much older man there's no sexual heat. But sometime late in the prolonged rehearsal period, Julianne and the decades-older George showed us that sometimes age doesn't make a difference and that the relationship can be quite passionate and hot. In rehearsal one day, they kissed. And kissed. And kissed. It was a breakthrough, one that took months over a period of years to get to. The professor's young wife was actually turned on by the old guy. We never would have discovered that in the usual, four-week rehearsal period. It may seem like a small discovery, but in a production filled with this kind of epiphany, it produces a richness, texture, and depth that you can't find in a more conventional process.

EUGENE LEE, who had by then been my designer for nearly thirty years, called. Eugene didn't know we were working on *Vanya*; he was just calling to show me what he called "a truly wonderful space." He had found it for something Harold Prince was directing, but Prince hadn't liked the space: the ruins of the old New Amsterdam Theatre on 42nd Street.

I met him there, in this magnificent ruin of a grand old theater. I loved it so much that I went back to the *Vanya* company and suggested we hold twelve run-throughs there to celebrate the *end* of our work. We could invite seven loved ones, one for each member of the company, have a supper for them afterward, and call it a day. Our work would be over.

We were uncertain about what we'd accomplished and had barely gotten through the final act. When our loved ones came to see it, though, they said it would be sinful to keep it from a larger audience. But we had an agreement; it would never be done for an audience. So what to do?

We finally decided we would do more open run-throughs, five a week, the following November and beginning of December, and each of us could invite three friends to each. This brought the audience for each performance up to a staggeringly large twenty-one. Once no one could get in to see it, the word spread like wildfire. A movie star, for example, would be in town from California, and ask his agent what to see. There's this underground *Vanya*, he'd be told, that's supposed to be amazing, but you can't get in. Because they couldn't get in, people would move mountains to see it. We were mobbed with requests.

Against all logic, design, and intention, we had a hit. By the time we had stopped performing, a grand total of 900 people had seen the show.

AFTER ONE OF THE PERFORMANCES, my friend Avedon asked Nichols if he liked what he saw. "Yes," Mike said. "Very, very good; it'll be interesting to see what happens when the actors begin to move around." Avedon, knowing my work, said he had a hunch the actors would never move around. "That's impossible," Mike said. "Actors always move around." I heard the ending to this delightful story much later: The following summer Nichols bumped into Jerome Robbins at a vegetable stand in the Hamptons. Nichols asked Robbins if he'd seen *Vanya*. Yes, Robbins told him; he'd loved it. "Isn't it great?" the legendary choreographer exclaimed. "The actors *never move!*"

ONE NIGHT VOLKER SCHLÖNDORFF, the German film director, came to see *Vanya*. In his thick German accent, he said something like, "Vot a vonderful space. I love this space. How amazing. What an amazing space. I love it." "I love it, too," I replied. "But what do you find so amazing about it?"

He gave the most amazing answer: "Here on this run-down street was the old Forty-second Street, the streets filled with pimps and whores and hustlers. A street of no culture in a nation which now has no culture. We enter the ruins of the theater, also destroyed, on the ruins of the street in the ruins of this country.

In this huge empty theater, empty seats once filled with tens of thousands of cultivated theatergoers, who would come to see something like this every night. And here on this abandoned, destroyed stage a small group of actors still believe in performing *Vanya*."

AFTER THAT BRIEF but glorious run, Chiquita and I returned to California. In the following months it became clear that the chemotherapy wasn't working. It had been about three years since she was diagnosed. She quickly deteriorated. Up to this point, she'd had little pain. Now she began to feel it. The doctor thought she had the flu. She went to the osteopath for her back pain, treatment she found unbearable. I told him how painful she had found it. "There was nothing I could do," he told me. "There was almost nowhere I could touch; the cancer is all through the body." Chiquita missed her friends and wanted them near. So we flew back to New York, and within a week she was gone.

25

LATE IN CHEKHOV'S *Three Sisters*, in the original version of the script, the doctor character says to Andrey, the brother of the three sisters of the title, "Tell me about your marriage." Andrey describes his marital problems. The doctor listens and responds: "If I were you, young man, I would put on your hat, grab your walking stick, head down that road, and never come back." Stanislavski, who directed all four of Chekhov's major plays for his seminal Moscow Art Theatre, told Chekhov that he felt the script wasn't explicit enough about Andrey's marital problems. Chekhov rewrote the scene with a long, long speech full of detail and discord. Too much, Stanislavski told him. Chekhov returned to his desk and came up with the final version, the one now in the play. The doctor says, "Tell me about your marriage," and Andrey replies, "What can I tell you? It's a marriage."

What can I tell you about my marriage to Chiquita, the quality and taste of life with the woman I shared it with for thirty-three years?

I have few memories of our marriage before she became ill. What I do remember gets overtaken by images from her cancer years.

I *remember* the time we spent together during the run of my first Off Broadway play more than fifty years ago. The two of us, night after night until dawn, loading buckets of paste and stacks of posters into the car and putting the posters up all over the city, illegally, laughing and joking as we did it.

I *remember* soon after our daughter, Marina, was born, waking early in a little beach house we had rented with my two brothers. The bed was empty, so I walked onto the porch. Chiquita was staring out to sea, her breast bare, feeding that lovely, tiny girl, as the red sun rose over the water. Filled with love, I watched this nativity scene and thought, *There must be a god.*

I *remember* a letter she wrote from Germany, where she visited her father before he died, to introduce to him his first grandson, Nick. She was devastated, she wrote, because Nick didn't love her. How in the world could an infant not love his mother?

I *remember* she called me "*mon soldat.*" I was her soldier, and she was mine. She wrote it in her last letter to me, which I had framed but now can't find. Our other nickname for each other, "Voosom," didn't really mean anything. Silly but sweet.

I *remember* a night in Afghanistan, before the endless wars there. We were able to visit because it was so close to Iran, where *Alice* would soon perform. We rode a horse and carriage through the dark, deserted streets of Kandahar. It was unusual, then, to travel anywhere without a guard. Suddenly, we were sure we would be killed. She grabbed my hand and her sharp nails drew blood.

I *remember* Dr. Yin sticking a long needle into her breast. She fainted from the pain. When she woke, the doctor confirmed our fears: She had cancer and would need a mastectomy. She went white. Terrified, yes, doubly so. In those days cancer still spelled death. And the surgery itself terrified her; she'd always been so proud of the beauty of her breasts. "No problem. Don't worry," the doctor consoled her. He opened his shirt and revealed his own chest. "It's nothing. Afterwards you'll look as good as me." I held her, sobbing, for a long time. Our lives had changed.

I *remember* checking into a Boston hotel. Chiquita was scheduled for a lumpectomy at Mass General. We were surprised by a large bouquet of flowers in the room, a gift from friends. We held each other. We were both afraid. We went down to the hotel pool. Chiquita didn't like to swim, but she was so nervous and scared, she swam what felt like a thousand laps that quiet Sunday afternoon. Two days later, after her surgery, we stood in the rain waiting for a cab. The doorman gripped my elbow and, as he squeezed, said, "Don't worry, kid, she'll be fine." I have never forgotten his kindness—a reminder to be kind, even to strangers passing through our lives.

Early on, for our anniversary, I sent her a large bouquet of gladiolas. How she loved them! So I sent them every anniversary, year after year. About a quarter of a century into married life, she awkwardly confessed, "You know what? I hate gladiolas, and I always have hated them."

I *remember* how we loved to talk. We hardly ever stopped. Talked about politics, books, movies. We were always terrific friends and always extremely supportive of the other's desires and needs. We were not so much husband and wife as brother and sister, Hansel and Gretel, two terrified children desperately holding hands, alone in a frightening wood, always ready for the big bad wolf. We talked about our terrible childhoods, how neither of us had received any love. We had both fled war and been raised by unstable parents with their own share of buried trauma. We even talked about that. We didn't, though, talk about the most important thing: what was going on between us.

Two people can dig a hole for themselves, a hole of silence and evasion, and after time goes by, the hole is too deep. You no longer know the name of the hole and you can no longer dig yourself out. Relationship—the idea that a couple would talk to each other about hidden truths, concerns, and fears—wasn't yet a widespread concept. You just swept unpleasant truths under the carpet.

In relationships as in art, it is not talent that matters much. It is tenacity. An artist cannot survive or grow without tenacity. And when you come from a privileged background, as I did, you don't learn about tenacity.

Chiquita and I stuck with it. In the fifties divorce wasn't an option. Also, we shared a lot—our love for Nicholas and Marina above all. The children brought extraordinary joy to our lives, and they continue to teach me—challenge me—to be a better human being. We loved many of the same things and, if we didn't talk about our "issues," we talked constantly about the world around us. As I launched my career she was unbelievably supportive, just as many years later, when she started her own career, I was supportive of her.

She had enormous courage. In her forties, wanting to work but having never held a job, she got a position at Bloomingdale's, selling dresses, a way of proving herself to herself. She became executive director of A Bunch of Experimental Theaters. Most important, Chiquita trained herself to direct films. She made two fine documentaries. The first, *Rings on the Water*, was a 1983 film about a group of Scandinavian women who marched from Stockholm to Moscow to protest nuclear weapons. Even though chronic back problems were causing her extreme pain, she went on the whole march, carrying her heavy camera. *Art as Vehicle*, her second film, was a documentary about the last stage of Grotowski's work. The film, which came out in 1990, is not only gorgeous, but is an essential document in the process of his development. And, of course, hers.

She became a sister to Grotowski. Even when he, too, was close to death and very fragile, he flew from his little village in Italy to Los Angeles to be by her bedside at the hospital where she lay dying. He would be one of the pallbearers at her funeral.

I HAVE OFTEN THOUGHT that we stayed together because, in some unconscious way, Chiquita reminded me of my mother, and I reminded her of her own. We had work to do together. Though I had never seen any physical resemblance between Chiquita and my mother, in her dying days Marina and I both noticed Chiquita's hands fluttering exactly the way my mother's hands would.

A PRIEST, UNANNOUNCED, came into her hospital room and asked if she wanted last rites. She didn't. She didn't like the Catholic Church anymore. She realized from his visit, though, that she was about to die. Ever a fifties couple, we had never been able to talk about her illness. "Am I going to die?" she asked me, as I entered her hospital room. "Yes, I think so." "I'm so blessed," she said. "I have such a lovely family."

THE FILM STAR CARMEN MIRANDA was a good friend of Chiquita's mother. When Chiquita was two or three years old, the three spent a beach holiday together in Rio. Women on the beach carried great parcels on their heads containing wares they had for sale. Chiquita would follow them, imitating their wiggles and waggles. Carmen Miranda, to egg Chiquita on, shouted, "Chica Chica Chica, boom boom boom." And so was born the Chiquita Banana song. At a party celebrating our thirtieth anniversary, an unforgettable group of beautiful women musicians, dressed in white tie and tails, played it on mostly brass instruments. For Chiquita's funeral our son, Nick, had the idea to have these same beautiful women, dressed in white tie and tails, play "Chiquita Banana" as the coffin was carried up the aisle and out of the church: a New Orleans–style funeral band playing a South American ditty on the Upper East Side.

26

AFTER CHIQUITA'S DEATH I was alone for the very first time in my life. I spent an awful nine months grieving with nothing to relieve the grief. I grew so lonely that I called the *Vanya* actors to see if they would work with me for another eight weeks the following summer, once again for a really small audience. They were game. They would do it. For me.

When that summer ended, I phoned Louis Malle in Paris. I knew he was frail. He had been ill, had undergone open-heart surgery. But I asked anyway. Might he reconsider? Yes, he said. If I could raise half a million dollars in three weeks he would shoot our *Vanya*. He flew to New York to catch our last run-through. The day before he arrived, Ruth Nelson had a heart attack and went blind. We cast one of Ruth's dearest friends from the Group Theatre, the dazzling Phoebe Brand, in Ruth's role.

All would come together, despite the odds, if I could raise half a million dollars in three weeks.

I TURNED TO A HINDU MYSTIC. Her name was Mother Meera and she lived in the woods in Germany. I had read a little booklet of hers. It said something like: "When you come to Mother come as you would on Christmas Eve. Don't ask for the large things like enlightenment or surrender. Ask as you would your own mother for what you want in your Christmas stocking." It might seem strange for a Hindu mystic to use Western Christmas imagery, but I didn't think about that. I rushed to Germany with about ten days left before filming was supposed to start.

You visited Mother Meera in a tiny, ugly lower-middle-class house in the woods. Very ordinary. Fifty of us were crammed together, waiting in the living room. When it was my turn to meditate with Mother, I knelt before her. She put her hands on my temples and looked into my eyes. I thought to myself: *I would like half a million dollars, a good therapist for my daughter, and a hot Saturday night date.* (It had been some time since Chiquita's death.)

COMING BACK FROM GERMANY, on a layover in Paris, I sat in a Left Bank café reading a book. An extremely attractive Frenchwoman sat at the next table, writing. I was too shy to open a conversation, so I kept on reading. Suddenly, there was a hand on my arm. *Hers.* "What do you think I am writing?" she asked. I had no idea. "I am translating a new play of Wally Shawn's," she told me. We spent three wonderful nights and days together.

The Manhattan Project on tour in Italy, 1971: so happy, we thought it would never end

BELOW: Gerry Bamman and Angela Pietropinto in Shiraz, Iran, 1971

Unless otherwise noted, all photographs are courtesy of the author.

My first day in
the Polish forest

My eleventh day in the Polish forest

With Jerzy Grotowski

Peter Pan in
Lotusland

When the Mouth was a little girl she had asthma. She had to stay in bed and smoke long, black asthma cigarettes that the Wizard gave her. Oliver would race over after school to watch.

Dior Women's Furs and Men's Clothing & Outerwear

Women's Jewelry, Legwear and Footwear.
Men's Dress Shirts, Neckwear, Scarves,
Mufflers and Eyewear.
Eau Sauvage.

Christian Dior

My brief life as a model

(PHOTOGRAPHS BY RICHARD AVEDON,
© THE RICHARD AVEDON FOUNDATION)

Meet the Diors: the Wizard, the Mouth, and Oliver.

Christian Dior

Dior for Men: Footwear, Hosiery, Sportshirts, Beachwear, Scarves & Mufflers, Gloves, Clothing & Outerwear, Ready-to-Wear, Dress Shirts, Neckwear, Underwear, Accessories, Nightwear, Eyewear, Sweaters, Robes, Loungewear & Activewear, Umbrellas.

Dior for Women: Furs, Intimate Apparel, Robes, Intimates, Scarves, Small Leather Goods, Jewelry, Gloves, Knit Hats & Mufflers, Footwear, Sportswear, Separates, Handbags & Luggage, Umbrellas & Rain Hats, Eyewear, Beachwear, Belts, Legwear, Activewear, Bed Linens.

Christian Dior Fragrances for Men & Women.
Christian Dior Makeup.

Like all good things, one Dior leads to another.

We've been talking for half a century... On the set of *My Dinner with André* with Wally Shawn
(PHOTO CREDIT: DIANA MICHENER)

On the set of *Vanya on 42nd Street* with Louis Malle and Julianne Moore
(WITH PERMISSION OF THE VANYA COMPANY)

With Jonathan Demme on the set of *A Master Builder*

With Debbie Eisenberg, Larry Pine, and Wally Shawn in an abandoned men's club on Wall Street: *The Designated Mourner*

Portrait of an artist — An early André drawing

André and Cindy on the Chiredzi River in Zimbabwe, 2019
(PHOTO CREDIT: CINDY KLEINE)

When I got back to New York, the money started pouring in. More than we needed. I ultimately had to give $300,000 back. Meanwhile, Marina found an excellent therapist.

The world is a miraculous place.

THE FILMING OF *Vanya on 42nd Street* was an exquisite experience. Neither Louis nor I speak much when we work. We would do a take, Louis would look over at me, I would give either a thumbs-up or thumbs-down, and he would know what I was thinking. If a thumbs-down, we would simply shoot again and get it right.

Louis's genius lay in capturing the live, spontaneous-feeling event of our live, spontaneous-feeling production, which was really a rehearsal for a production. He didn't aim to make a film of Chekhov's *Vanya*. He filmed *our Vanya*, from the company's walk to the theater down 42nd Street through our act breaks and coffee breaks and exit from the theater afterward. Rather than transporting us visually to rural Russia, he kept us lodged right there in that magnificent, decrepit old theater, on benches or at a beaten table, in the living presence of a few friends of the actors, our tiny audience. For a film camera, as for so small an audience, stage actors don't have to "project" their voices. They don't have to *emote*. They can simply be. Louis caught them *being*.

AT TIMES DURING THE FILMING, I couldn't help but think of Ruth Nelson, who had died just before we started, and who had been with us from the start.

Ideally one's last word should be Ruth's. She had insisted on performing in *Vanya* even when she was very, very ill. We put a cot in her dressing room, and she asked us to wake her just before each entrance. And how she would enter! She took the stage with some inexplicable power, fueled by a lifetime of deep feeling and her unflinching dedication to truth. No one could look away.

I didn't like the thought of Ruth riding the bus to the theater, so one day I sent a car for her. She refused the ride and showed up as usual on the bus. "Dear, dear André. I'm a Marxist. Too late to change my ways." I visited her often in her final weeks. I even asked her to marry me. "Oh, dear, dear André, let's do it the next time around."

"Are you afraid of death?" I asked her. "Oh no," she answered. "Death is like our work: You just go moment to moment without thinking about what the result will be." I've been told that her last words were "Here we go," but, according to her son, she simply said, "Geronimo." The best last word ever.

CRITICS OFTEN EMPHASIZE THE BOREDOM in Chekhov's plays, but the plays are not about boredom. The word is hardly mentioned in *Uncle Vanya*. Nor are the plays about the Russian aristocracy, another popular misconception. The characters are ordinary people—soldiers, doctors, teachers, actors. Even the ones with money have money problems. The name Vanya means "Johnny" in Russian.

No, Chekhov writes about yearning—the very human error of yearning for what you can never have, instead of celebrating what you do have. Chekhov writes about what it is like to be *here*, on this earth, for the short time we have. What it *feels* like to live a life. We are given the lives we are given and must live them as best we can. We face inevitable pain with dignity.

· · ·

LEO TOLSTOY ONCE HONORED Chekhov with an invitation to lunch on the great Tolstoy's legendary estate. The giant of Russian letters told Chekhov how dearly he loved his short stories. He showered him with compliments, story by story. Then, over tea, Tolstoy said, "There is only one thing I would ask. Please, please, stop writing those awful and boring plays."

VANYA IS MY MOST AUTOBIOGRAPHICAL WORK. Everyone in the play corresponds to someone in my family. Serebryakov was my grandfather, Yelena my mother, Vanya my father, Sonya my Isee. Watching the film some years later I realized that every actor even looks like someone in my family. After World War II, you could go into our kitchen apartment almost any night, and my parents would be there, sitting together after some fashionable party, trying to decide whether or not to return to Europe. Always yearning for the home they'd lost. For what they didn't have.

THE FILM WAS TURNED DOWN by the New York Film Festival, which was remarkable since Wally and I were hometown boys and Louis was an international auteur. Nevertheless, the film made more than a million dollars. And the work that was never meant to be shown or seen became a modest film classic.

I SAW JERZY GROTOWSKI only once after Chiquita died. He came to Chicago to renew his green card, and I screened *Vanya* for him and his dramaturg. Later, I heard that Jerzy, who had lived with leukemia for years, was growing more and more frail.

I wanted to visit, but I was frightened to see him, diminished and dying. I was overwhelmed with my own grief. I didn't know what to do. I had heard from his associates in Italy that he no longer wanted to see anyone. I sent him a long, long letter, full of love. I had heard that he didn't want visitors while he was dying, which was fine with me, because I didn't want to watch him die. But still I felt guilty. George Gaynes translated the letter into French. I apologized for letting him down in any way.

His answer was a telegram: "Je t'aime." I love you.

After Grotowski's death I had breakfast with the young dramaturg he'd brought to watch *Vanya on 42nd Street*. She recounted what Jerzy had told her when they left the screening: "You don't need to see any more theater. You don't need to read any more books on theater. See this film every day, and you will understand the nature of theater." You wait a lifetime to hear words like these from a brother, friend, mentor.

ABOUT A YEAR AFTER the film's completion Louis Malle himself died. At his memorial they played a clip of Wally as Vanya in his last scene with Brooke Smith, playing his niece Sonya. Her final, beautiful speech. "But what can we do. Uncle. All we can do is live. We'll live through a long row of days. And through the endless evenings. And we'll bear up. Under the trials fate has sent to us." Mike Nichols, who was sitting next to me, grabbed my hand, and we both wept as Brooke/Sonya concluded. "But wait. And only wait, Uncle Vanya, we shall rest. We shall rest."

27

CONSCIOUSLY OR NOT I was not comfortable being bitter or resentful. There was someone else in me, I knew, someone joyful and loving. I didn't know where to find this André, though. I hadn't yet met him. I would need a hammer and a blowtorch first, to rid myself of the defensive, angry young man, now approaching sixty.

I grew up in a world of private clubs, private schools, and debutante balls. I went to the best schools with privileged young boys who used their privilege to get into those fancy schools and, through the people they met there, to get the best jobs. They were the boys who became the men who ruled our country.

I am not proud to have been part of that world, but I'm proud of the work I've done to leave that world behind. Thousands of painful hours in a therapist's office. Years of studying Torah and Hebrew with rabbis. Months and months in the presence of my guru. How much chanting, and how much meditation? How many journeys, how many questions, how much frustration to deal with this task: to awaken one André inside the other?

AN ACTOR ONCE ASKED Grotowski what was most important for an actor to know. "One person is born Mr. Van Gogh and another Mr. X," Grotowski told him. "It's most important for one to live fully the life of Mr. Van Gogh and for the other to live fully the life of Mr. X."

PRIVILEGED MEN KNOW they can pay or charm their way out of anything. Living isolated in such a privileged world separates you from the world itself. I feel some shame about the money I was born into, but not about the work it allowed me to do. Though Wally and I have had to work and fund-raise hard to pay for every project we've done, my parents' money bought me the freedom to imagine and live this creative life. I am extremely lucky, because I believe in that life.

I DIDN'T BECOME A PART of the human race until I was faced with Chiquita's illness and death. Before then, empathy was an idea to me. I hadn't felt the suffering of others in my own body. Not knowing others, how could I know myself? I was born into the life of Mr. Gregory, but I had to learn to live it fully.

28

MY DAUGHTER, MARINA, led me to Gurumayi. Around the time of Chiquita's cancer diagnosis, we were vacationing on a tropical island when Chiquita woke up in the middle of the night screaming. She had had a nightmare in which Marina was being attacked and beaten. The following morning, Marina called. She had just returned from an emergency room in L.A., where she'd been treated for multiple bruises. A fellow acting student had gone over the edge in rehearsal and tried to strangle her.

Terrified, Marina went to work at a trauma center. There, manning the phones, helping others, she learned of a nearby meditation center and its guru. Suddenly, our daughter was chanting at sunrise, chanting at sunset, chanting in the bath, mumbling prayers before breakfast, covering her bedroom walls with pictures of a gorgeous guru, and fingering white prayer beads nonstop: "Om Namah Shivaya . . . Om Namah Shivaya . . . Om . . . Om . . . Om." Chiquita and I found it silly and annoying. The prayers from her bedroom wouldn't stop.

Despite my inexplicable encounters with the inexplicable, this stuff was not for me. I didn't believe in gurus. I didn't believe in a god. I didn't believe in prayer.

Marina begged us to join her at the ashram for her birthday, which is, coincidentally, on the same day as her guru's. I really did not want to go. But I went to make Marina happy. We stood in line for the guru's blessing: a bop on the head with peacock feathers. God, how ridiculous!

When I reached Gurumayi, however, it was as if joy and love had permeated me. I took her hand—something you don't do with a guru—put it on my heart, and said, "I don't know what to do. I am in such pain. My wife is very ill." She put her hand over mine, smiled, and said, "Come back to us in the fall. It will be quieter then."

I stood before the most loving, luminous woman I had ever met. I was drowning in love. And so began my love for the guru who walked with me through Chiquita's death and beyond.

THE MAJOR ONGOING CRY in *My Dinner with André* is "Wake up! Wake up!" That cry has been the goal of my work ever since.

I flew to Gurumayi's ashram immediately after Chiquita's funeral. I had been there for a few days when, one night, I had what felt like an epileptic fit. I was shaking. It was hard to talk—I mostly stuttered. I rushed to Marina's room and told her—in halting words—how terrified I was. "Oh, you are so blessed," she replied. "You've received Shaktipat."

I didn't care what I had received; I just wanted this awful trembling to stop. Marina took me by the hand. She led me to this very lovely monk, who explained that Shaktipat is a process by which one's entire system is shocked awake. It is as if you are driving a car through a blizzard, he explained. The windshield is covered with ice, the wipers don't work, and the guru comes with a warm cloth and wipes the windshield clean. You are finally able to see, and you see with a clarity you have never known before.

And the shaking? I asked. The shaking, he said, is caused by the shit of your lifetime pouring out of every orifice, even the shit accumulated from lives you've lived before. This purging is necessary for you to see. "It is a blessing," he said. "It is as if you awaken from a long sleep."

SHAKTIPAT IS A TECHNIQUE HANDED DOWN from guru to guru over generations. They learn how to wake us in this way. I assume that this is what happened when the Rinpoche of Ladakh turned the daytime sky black, and I roared with laughter and wept so wildly. Gurumayi, too, has been giving Shaktipat. When you chant with Gurumayi, you have what feels like hour-long orgasms. You laugh so hard you think you will die. They are orgasmic, ecstatic explosions. Once, in a chanting session, I was so over the top, the guru shouted, "Get that gentleman a seat belt."

Gurumayi once said, "Everything is funny, even death. I have seen death, and I know: he is very, very funny." I hope she's right. When I listened to the radio during World War II, listened to the news of battles overseas, I hoped I would have courage when I was called to fight. These days I hope I have the courage to laugh when I meet the guru's jolly friend.

29

BY THE TIME I was sixty—*only* sixty, as I now think of it—
my wife and dearest friend had already died. Every man I
knew was talking about his prostate. I was no exception and, ultimately, I had surgery to shrink mine. They stuck a 35-mm camera
up my penis—well, not quite that large—to get a picture. The surgeon invited me to watch. "No thanks," I answered in pain. "This
is not one of my favorite movies."

BY THEN, TOO, my teeth, from lack of care, had become so rotten that my dentist prescribed implants. It took six years and cost
a fortune, but now there's not a real tooth in my head. It was an

excruciating experience. The dentist kept saying, "I don't know why you feel so much pain; none of my other patients do." Other dentists tell me he was full of shit. One night, in spite of painkillers, I begged to be taken to the ER and knocked out.

BY YOUR SEVENTIES other men stop talking about their prostates and start talking about their knees. My arthritic right knee, for instance, sometimes buckles under me. This is the time, as a friend put it, "of the body's little betrayals."

And big betrayals. A week never passes without a call from a friend helping a loved one through some awful, debilitating treatment for some awful, debilitating illness. I feel like a World War I soldier, crouching in the trenches, shells whizzing overhead, pulling my helmet over my face and praying that the next bullet won't get me.

WHEN I SHAVE, I try not to look at my face. At the gym the other day, though, I caught sight of myself in the mirror and, without thinking, said, "Oh my god, I look like an old widow at a crime scene."

IT WAS MY BROTHER PETER, as I've said, who called this the age of You're-looking-great! (He's a natty dresser, so the phrase truly applies to him.) Peter and I hardly knew each other earlier in life. He is nine years younger, which made a huge difference. I'm not sure we even liked each other.

One day, maybe twenty years ago, a family therapist he was working with called me and said she thought Peter needed an older brother. I should call him once in a while. I phoned him once a week at his office where he is an investment banker. It became a few times a week. Now it is almost every day.

We talk about our therapy. We talk about books and send as gifts the ones we think the other might like. We talk about the state of the world. We have lunch together as often as we can.

He is a wonderful husband, father, and grandfather, besotted by his granddaughter. He's been a guardian angel to our brother Alexis, as Alexis's health has declined.

Age has brought Peter and me close together. We are the dearest of friends.

UNTIL OUR LATE TWENTIES, when our lives went in different directions, Alexis, only two years younger than me, was my closest friend. We went to the same schools, even rooming together in college. As teenagers, we traveled alone together through Europe. He scoured museums. I looked for girlfriends. In every picture of us as children, my arm is wrapped protectively around his shoulders. He looks fragile, like a scrawny Jewish violinist. Even then, he looked old.

Alexis loved music. He attended the opera and Carnegie Hall and even put together a chamber group of his own. A few years out of college, he would play the piano for Chiquita and me over the phone. In his later years, he created an international competition to help pianists in their careers.

And he lived—still lives—for art. Alexis could have been a great museum curator, but my father bullied him out of it. "You won't make any money," he argued.

I must have sensed his isolation, but we drew apart. He was always hidden and didn't share his life with me. I didn't know about his sadness or relationships. I knew only that he stayed close to our parents, while I got away. And that he made a lot of money.

I made my life in the theater, and he made theater of his life, not unlike our parents did, surrounding himself with fascinating people. For his seventieth birthday he invited two hundred friends to Venice. The guests danced to two orchestras in a grand palazzo on the Grand Canal. Gondoliers picked us up at our hotels, their gondolas decorated by flaming torches, taking us to a palazzo lit by flaming torches, where an acrobat juggled flaming torches.

He, too, is in his eighties now, and he still lives in a spacious apartment just like our parents' home, filled with his art and their ornate furniture, where he even entertained several of their ancient friends. Nick and Peter and I still visit him, but for the most part, the parties now are over. It reminds me of Shakespeare's *The Tempest*, a play I think of more and more.

> *And, like the baseless fabric of this vision,*
> *The cloud-capped towers, the gorgeous palaces,*
> *The solemn temples, the great globe itself,*
> *Yea, all which it inherit, shall dissolve,*
> *And, like this insubstantial pageant faded,*
> *Leave not a rack behind.*

Alexis is forthcoming about his pain in a way he never was before, and while still unknown to me, he is, after all, my little brother. Always was, always will be.

AFTER *VANYA* ALL my productions have been about death. When I embarked on Ibsen's *A Master Builder* in 1997, for example, I didn't look at the play as one about how you choose to die, which it partly is; to me it was a confessional play about my feelings of inadequacy as a family man. By the time we were finishing the production in 2011 and '12, I was thinking about eternity.

I came down with pneumonia. The X-rays showed that I also had lymphoma. I didn't know what lymphoma was, believe it or not, until a friend, during an act break, cried out, "Lymphoma? Oh my god, that's cancer!" I couldn't believe it. I had cancer. A few weeks before our invited rehearsals began, I called my internist for advice. I was not only directing and producing the Ibsen through its final stages, but I was performing in it. Was this insane? "That's something I simply can't answer," she replied. "You have to answer that for yourself. You know your own capacities. I can't tell you to do it, and I can't tell you not to."

I postponed our first open rehearsals by a week and went into training. I had no energy. Every day I would begin a modest walk through Greenwich Village to get in shape, to build up some tiny bit of stamina. First one block, then three blocks, then eight blocks, a little rest on a quiet park bench, and home again to rest. We performed *A Master Builder*. By day I played a dying man, old Brovik, after spending the morning at the hospital getting biopsies and other tests. I knew that if we didn't do the play then, we never would.

NO IMAGINATION WAS REQUIRED to play old Brovik. I had learned what it was to stare at death. Every time we did a take, I would just think for a moment about getting biopsied, about my diagnosis. Just for a moment. Then I would let the lines fall into my psyche like a pebble into a pool. But after each take, I'd lock myself in the men's room and sob uncontrollably.

. . .

RABBI GELBERMAN, at age ninety, said that he woke every morning with pain in his joints, pain in his neck, pain in his knees, and so on. When he showered, he would shampoo his head and say, "Thank you, God, for my hair." He would shampoo his chest and say, "Thank you, God, for my heart."

APPROACHING EIGHTY WAS REALLY DEPRESSING. There was no way to pretend this was still middle age. I've read that the Buddha believed we are always in a state of bliss or ecstasy. Three things get in the way of that ecstasy: rage, envy, and illusion. Normally, that would have seemed like religious gobbledygook. Suddenly I thought, *Oh yes, I get it. I'm in a* rage *about getting older. I* envy *everyone who is younger. And I live with the* illusion *that I can live forever.* Since reading that, my eighties feel just fine.

Entering your eighties is not so different from graduating college. You face a new, uncertain decade, and you have to figure out the best way to live through that decade. What to do with these ten years? You hope ten. Of course, the question will answer itself.

YEARS AGO MY FRIENDS and I talked about sex and ambition; now we talk about illness and death. We discuss books on dying, on the chaos of hospitals, the mediocrity of doctors and the indifference of health care. Increasingly, though, this death talk turns to end-of-the-world talk—global warming, the approaching flooding of our cities, Cape Cod houses sliding into the ocean. The wealthy have staffed ships waiting on the Hudson for their escape. We worry that if the nuclear plant across the bay south of Boston explodes we will be trapped on Cape Cod. There is only one road off the Cape, but you can get free pills at the Town Hall in Provincetown that offer 24-hour protection from nuclear radiation. Our friends have these pills.

If this end-of-days talk is any indication, we are living in the most terrifying era since the early 1930s, the rise of Hitler and Stalin. How did my parents and their generation make sense of the approaching horrors? What were their conversations then? How did the Jews know when it was time to trade the known life—a lovely house, maybe—for an unknown future, a future that may or may not take place? How did my father stay one step ahead of the chaos? Nothing happens the way you think it will.

If death is all around us, how should we live? How do we find hope in the darkness?

I believe—and this is very, very important to emphasize—that love is all, love of others, love of self, and even, perhaps, love of the process of letting go of life.

A MASTER BUILDER ends with a once-great architect lured to climb to the top of a tower he has built—as he did in his younger, more nimble days—to crown that tower with a wreath. It's a climb he should never have made, but he does. He falls to his death. Or does he leap? That's the final question of this mysterious play: how to leap joyously into the terrifying unknown. This is the example of Ruth Nelson: *Geronimo.*

30

THERE'S A HASIDIC TALE I LOVE. It seems that way back in the eighteenth century a wealthy man from a tiny village in Poland went on a long journey to visit and learn from a holy rabbi, a great rabbi. Many months later, when he returned to his own village, the townspeople crowded around and asked him what he had learned, what the rabbi had said. "Oh," answered the wealthy man, "if he said anything I've forgotten what it was. But it is amazing how much I learned."

"What did you learn?" they asked.

"I learned everything he had to teach from watching the way he tied his shoes."

A similar thing happened to me. Some years ago when I was leading a workshop in Jerusalem, one of my students asked me if I would like to meet a great teacher. He took me to a tiny little hummus shop, and we sat for lunch. "Where was the holy man?" I asked when we had left. "He was the man making the hummus," answered my student. "The lesson is in the way he stirs the hummus."

AS PICASSO PUT IT, "It takes a very long time to become young."

YEARS PASSED. Chiquita was gone. I'd taken numerous visits to Gurumayi's ashram. Marina had nearly married a fellow ashramite, a Jewish artist from Russia named André. Marina suggested I attend a singles dance at the ashram. No way. No way. My daughter felt I'd been alone too long. She offered to burn a prayer stick in Shiva's flame, asking Shiva for a new wife for me. I didn't really want to remarry, and I didn't know what a prayer stick was. *It's a thin piece of wood on which you write your prayers*, she told me. *You burn it in the sacred flame.*

Nick and Marina were both grown up and deep into their own lives. Nick was acting in films and directing; Marina was fully involved at the ashram. Nothing was keeping me from getting on with my own life. Maybe my daughter was right: I needed a companion.

Why not? Would I want to share my life with an artist? Sure. Would it be nice if she could cook? Of course. What if we lived in the same neighborhood? Why not? A bit younger? Absolutely. A big heart? Oh yes, yes. I wrote all of it on a sliver of pale wood, and we threw it in the flames. Three days later I met Cindy. I would finally learn the art of loving.

WE HAD EVERYTHING IN COMMON, including our favorite filmmaker, Andrei Tarkovsky, our zip code, and our underlined copies of Alice Miller's *Drama of the Gifted Child*, the finest book I have ever read on child rearing—all about loving our children for who they truly are, not for who we need and want them to be. No wonder we were reading it; our parents could have tied for gold in the Olympics of bad parenting. We loved the same movies, the same books. We laughed at the same things.

Cindy and I went out for dinner in Sag Harbor, in the Hamptons, on New York's Long Island. We talked until sunrise—about our awful families, about therapy, about the world, about love. She was working, at that time, on *Til Death Do Us Part*, a short film about her parents' abysmal fifty-year marriage, which would later become the feature-length *Phyllis and Harold*. Both films were acclaimed in the documentary world and are examples of how Cindy, a transgressive and radical filmmaker and artist, is able to make moving, profound, and, at times, hilarious art out of her own personal history. Her passion, her calling, and her bold humor in the face of chaos made me love her, almost instantly.

I told her all I could about my marriage to Chiquita. There was no danger, though, of this turning into a romance. Cindy was twenty-four years younger, which made everything more relaxed. We would just be friends. And we were. We remained *just friends* for three days.

. . .

TWO NIGHTS LATER I dreamed we were standing on a street corner, kissing. Right before she was about to leave the Hamptons for Manhattan, I told Cindy I had dreamed about her. She was embarrassed, but the friend she was with wanted to hear the dream. So I told them. Cindy blushed. Her friend slipped out to the car. As if on cue we said, in unison, "It ain't a street corner, but it'll do." We kissed. She fled the house and set off for the city. I left a message on her home answering machine to greet her: "I have been looking through law books and found an ancient law that says it's a felony to kiss and run."

We have never broken that law again.

I LOVE THE POWERFUL, weird, and wonderful films Cindy makes. We both adore film. She brought into my life the work of European filmmakers such as Terence Davies, Abbas Kiarostami, Theodoros Angelopoulos, Jacques Rivette, Robert Bresson, and the Michelangelo of film, Andrei Tarkovsky. I brought her the great American studio directors of the thirties and forties.

Cindy and I are both talkers, and we love to laugh. I doubt you can have a great relationship without great laughter. When I had lymphoma Cindy went to a Broadway costume rental shop and outfitted herself with a nurse's uniform. She became "The Naughty Nursie" and took naughty selfies with her patient. Her performance helped us through that terrifying time. We laughed our way through, me and Nursie. She's my own private Borscht Belt comic.

And she makes me laugh at myself. There's a terrific moment in her 2014 film about my life, my work, and our marriage, *André Gregory: Before and After Dinner*. Throughout the film she presents herself as a seeker and artist with a long trail of former boyfriends behind her. Meanwhile, she builds me up as the "great man," the wise man, the theater guru. Then she pulls the carpet out from under the audience (and me) by shooting me naked, with all my old guy wrinkles, in a shower cap, waving happily and shyly at the camera.

CINDY GAVE ME SOMETHING they say you can't have in American life: a second act. As of this writing, we've been married for twenty years.

Strangely, even with our age difference, I have always felt younger, like a graduate student with an older woman. The age difference is real, though, and so the two issues we confronted early on were children—whether to have them—and abandonment, as I was almost certain to die first. I didn't want another child. I had two, and they were grown. I didn't want to be eighty-five when my kid began college. Cindy thought about it a lot and wasn't sure. She finally decided she was okay not having children. Instead, we had cats. If you haven't had pets, you can't know how deeply we love them. Our beloved cats are the stars of Cindy's new film, *Dead Girl Vampire Cats*. I sometimes wonder, who will live longer, the cats or me?

AS FOR AGE AND ABANDONMENT: The odds in Vegas are against me, and Cindy is terrified I will go before she does. I'm terrified that I will go, period. I understand her fear. If she died first, I would want to throw myself on a funeral pyre and burn to ashes. I know how hard it is to find Ms. Right. I met an astrologer who had never been in love. At age seventy-nine she was hired to do astrological readings on an Adriatic cruise. She and the ship's eighty-year-old captain fell instantly in love. They married on board during the crossing. "You know," she told me, "it might have been nice if it had happened sooner, but I feel blessed that it happened at all."

AND SO WE TELL OURSELVES to be grateful that we're together, that we found each other, that we've had these precious, fun, transformative years. I have two dear friends, a couple, who live on Hawaii; both are very close to dying. I called them on Christmas Day, and they told me they had had a wonderful holiday. They did nothing but sit together all day, holding hands and feeling grateful. We must not, as they say in Alcoholics Anonymous, live in the wreckage of the future.

Speaking of wreckage, when I confront Cindy with this aging face and ask if it looks like an elephant stepped on it, she tells me with complete conviction that I look young and handsome. When my creaky knees stop me from keeping pace with her on the street, she compares me to a gorgeous old custom Studebaker. Yes, the fine old leather on the front seat is cracked. Yes, some kid stole the rearview mirror. Yes, some air has leaked out of the tires, and yes, only one of the window wipers works. But boy oh boy, look how that old roadster *tears* up the highway!

Every day Cindy teaches me how to move beyond myself to love another. I think of Rilke's extraordinary statement, "Once the realization is accepted that even between the closest human beings infinite distances continue, a wonderful living side by side can grow, if they succeed in loving the distance between them which makes it possible for each to see the other whole against the sky." Today, Cindy is in her office, editing her newest installation, making an eccentric horror movie out of our beloved cats. I'm painting away in my studio. We meet again in the kitchen, make tea, reach into the cabinet for a snack. We live in that wonderful "side by side," a kind of romantic parallel play, and then through talk and story and laughter we bridge the infinite distance, seeing each other "whole against the sky."

Some nights by the light of the Cape moon, I look over at her in our bed, head poking up from the spring green earth of the sheets like a lovely, curly little cabbage, and I think, "*My god*, how I adore her."

CINDY HAS UNIFIED ME. I am no longer a Jekyll and Hyde, living one life uptown and another in my downtown art. My anger lifted, and friends marveled at its absence. (Until the 2016 election.) She has swept away much of my darkness and replaced it with a sense of calm. I can now live my life the way I make my art—out of love.

31

I AM A STORYTELLER with many stories to tell, but I'd resisted the urgings of friends to write them down. I didn't want
to write a memoir. I'd never kept a diary or preserved letters. I wasn't
interested in the past. I preferred the present, especially in this blissful time of life. At loose ends, though, I spent a week with a good
young writer and began to tell my tale. No good. I didn't like it.

Over lunch one day, I said to Cindy, out of nowhere, "You
know, if I could do anything in the world, I would draw. But I'd
never have the nerve. Too hard." I still don't know where the idea
came from. When I told my new idea to the young writer, she mentioned a friend she'd met at the MacDowell Colony, Tara Geer, a

fine artist. Tara had boasted that she could teach an elephant how to draw. Soon Tara and the elephant were hard at work. We've been friends now, teacher and student, for over a decade. I could never have imagined, at the beginning, that one day my work would hang side by side with hers at a New York gallery.

WHEN CINDY FIRST BROUGHT ME to the Cape, I was overwhelmed by its beauty. We are sixty miles out to sea, surrounded by water, so the light changes by the minute—amazes by the minute. I stand on the Longnook dunes, overlooking an ocean reflecting the blue of the sky and the red of the great dunes. The water's azure and aquamarine mix with colors I've never seen before. I weep. Early in the morning I have coffee in Truro Center, which comprises a deli, post office, and fish store. I gaze at the light on the shingled buildings (pure Edward Hopper, who painted nearby) and, again, tears come to my eyes. This is why the Cape is filled with painters and poets and photographers. They come for the light.

I LEARNED TO DRAW SLOWLY. Look. Make a mark. Look. Make a mark. I never have an idea, a thought, of what it should look like finished. I have nothing in mind. That's the joy of beginner's mind, of learning again, of being a child. The joy of play. The joy of not giving it a thought. Of beginning at the beginning. Ecstasy!

Plays tend to be sad, dark things, at least the ones I've been drawn to. I would, of course, try to bring light to Shawn or Beckett, but painting is, for me, all light.

Moreover, it's so much easier to do. I don't have to find actors or keep them together. I needn't search for rehearsal space, or space in which to perform. I don't have to raise money to pay everybody or bring together a dozen disparate visions—the playwright's and actors' and designers'. No producer is telling me what to do. I can make what I want to make. I need only pencils, paints, and paper, tenacity and perseverance. And love for what I'm doing—without self-judgment. I feel myself returning to the André I was born to be.

Generally, as we age the world shrinks. Our creaky, arthritic knees won't carry us far. Travel gets rougher. Our friends begin to pass on. We age like Winnie in Beckett's *Happy Days*, buried up to the armpits in earth, surrounded by cosmetics and medications. A shrinking world, slowly burying us. But my world grew larger through painting, Cindy's gift to me. I am living a second childhood. At eighty-four years old, paintbrush in hand, I splash around in the Fountain of Youth.

Without the eyes of a painter, or a child, we look at trees and think: green. But *look*. Trees are so much more—black, yellow, red, umber. Depending on the light, all colors exist in everything. "Color," Paul Klee says, "links us with cosmic regions."

And shadows, shadows everywhere. Just look. And wonder. As I learn to look, the world appears richer, larger, more splendid. My wonder grows. Look at the shape of that bottle. See the hues in that fruit or the way pills in a vial knock against one another. Watch the spools on a movie projector. Entering my second childhood, I experienced a first childhood. A baby lies in a crib with a brightly colored mobile suspended above it, and the baby is mesmerized. How to capture this richness, this variety?

For a long time I drew old-fashioned, functional objects from a bygone era: obsolescent typewriters, telephones, film projectors. These were a kind of self-portrait, as an elderly André looked back with fond nostalgia at an André from another, earlier time. In the cracks and corners of these drawings you might find a goblin, wizard, or monster lurking. This is the child's-eye view, old man and young boy in the same picture.

Then I began actual self-portraits. Face after face after face. André dark, André light. André silly. Did they illuminate the real André? I don't think a single picture can do that. Look, make a mark, look, make a mark. The work is meditative and mindless. Some objects are harder than others. I've painted eyeglasses, faces, flowers, and landscapes. I tried to draw a bicycle, which was a catastrophe at first, unbelievably tricky. The perspective is really tough, and there are so many parts to it—chains and spokes and seat, wheels and wires. A good bike is very hard to do. Once I tried two together. I called it *Two Fuckin' Bicycles*. A friend sent me this, from the painter Camille Pissarro: "Blessed are those who see beautiful things in humble places where others see nothing."

ONE SPRING I PAINTED nearly fifty skulls. It started accidentally. Richard Baker (like Tara, a teacher and friend) had a skull on his table. Having nothing else to paint that day, I took a crack at the skull and couldn't stop. Skulls for months. Funny skulls, terrifying skulls, skulls in charcoal and in paint, skulls with swastikas, skulls with hair. One friend who'd seen them told another friend—they were both shrinks—how courageous I was to confront my own death so creatively. Now I wonder, was I intuiting the approach of Trump?

TO PAINT IS TO LOVE AGAIN is the title of a book Henry Miller wrote after he took up watercolors. And how right he was! To paint is to love again. During my years in the "desert," after the breakup of the Manhattan Project, having abandoned my vocation or been abandoned by it, Miller's radical action—throwing over fiction for painting—was for me a sign of hope. Would I dare? Could I muster the foolhardy courage to do something that radical? Might I leave theater behind forever?

"I remember well the transformation which took place in me when I first began to view the world with the eyes of the painter," Miller wrote. "The most familiar things, objects which I had gazed at all my life, now became an unending source of wonder, and with the wonder, of course, affection. A tea pot, an old hammer, a chipped cup, whatever came to hand I looked upon as if I had never seen it before. I hadn't, of course."

Late at night the novelist-turned-painter would visit his finished paintings in his studio. I do the same. While Cindy sleeps, I traipse out to the barn to visit my "grandchildren," as I've nick-named my drawings and paintings. Are they sleeping well? Do they need anything? Might one or another appreciate a little touch-up in the morning?

IN MY SEVENTIES, it was too late in life to worry about making a career as a visual artist or being part of a *scene*. It was too late to think about reviews or selling. I could give my work to friends, and I did. I would never be Matisse. So what? I could be more of André Gregory. And soon, through drawing after drawing and painting after painting, by looking and looking and making marks without a thought in my head, I found a new me. Rudolph Steiner wrote about the "karma of vocation." The vocation we find late in this life, he felt, might prepare us for our vocation in the next one.

I hope so.

· · ·

I HAVE TRAVELED THE WORLD to find great theater teachers. I have sat at their feet and watched their performances over and over. I have read all the great theater books. But a new world has opened before me in my twilight years: the Metropolitan Museum of Art and MoMA, the Frick and the Whitney, Dia: Beacon, the Barnes in Philadelphia, Chinati in the Texas desert, the Prado and Thyssen in Madrid, London's Portrait Gallery and Tate Modern, and all the galleries just blocks from where we live in Chelsea. I didn't enjoy looking at paintings before, because I didn't know *how* to look. Now I can't stop.

RECENTLY, AT THE THYSSEN in Madrid, marveling my way through room after room of astonishing paintings, a landscape at the far end of the gallery literally took my breath away. A watery, winter scene by Emil Nolde. I fixed on a small, white, skeletal bridge, covered with ice, crossing a small river running through marshland. I let out a quiet whoop of recognition. I felt as if I knew this image, had seen it before. It struck some deep chord in me—from the past, the present, the future. I knew I might never see it again, so, while in Madrid, I returned to it many times. To gaze on it with love.

I had lived in a world without the friendship of Matisse, Guston, de Kooning, Bosch, Vermeer, Sargent, Fra Angelico—the list goes on. They are now my family. Every artist I love—and I love so many—shows me another undiscovered side of myself. Like notes of a concerto, their brushstrokes, their paint—because painting is *about* paint—go straight to the heart and activate the soul. Theirs is the ecstasy of the new, the glory of seeing what's never been seen, the kaleidoscope of colors that melt and merge and make one another shine.

32

THE LITTLE PRINCE SAYS that one can only see rightly with the heart; "what is essential is invisible to the eye." I am an intuitive animal, and I don't ever really know what I am doing. When I draw I look at an object and make a mark. I think of nothing for hours at a time. After all that mindless looking and all those marks, something exists I would never have imagined. At the end, maybe, I get out my eraser for a little change here or there. Directing plays works like that, too. I don't intend. I don't *think*. But something happens, something unexpected.

The best description I've found of this kind of *seeing* appears in the psychiatrist Mark Epstein's *The Trauma of Everyday Life*.

The observational posture that Buddhist psychology counsels is sometimes called bare attention . . . Bare attention has been defined as the "clear and single-minded awareness of what happens to us and in us at the successive moments of perception." In the Tibetan Buddhist tradition, this is sometimes evoked through the setting up of what is called a spy consciousness in the corner of the mind, watching or feeling everything that unfolds in the theatre of the mind and body.

Epstein exactly captures what I experience in rehearsals. When I watch actors rehearse, I concentrate so intensely on each actor that there is total inner silence. I don't locate the center of being in any particular moment of rehearsal, this performance, or that event. I don't "concentrate" or focus on myself. All my concentration is on the actors. I assume that tennis champions, surgeons, and painters—certainly this painter—labor in this exact state.

It's a strange thing to rehearse for years at a time, while sitting and saying almost nothing, thinking almost nothing.

I LOVE THE WAY Simone Weil nails it: "Absolute unmixed attention is prayer." I have no idea where I learned to *attend* in this way, though I could hazard a guess. I grew up like a spy in my parents' house, silently assessing their *text*. What were they really saying? What were they really thinking? Like Avedon staring through the little hole in the black drape to his bedroom, artists are spies. We are also collectors of other people's garbage. Or maybe that wasn't it at all. Maybe I learned this bare, concentrated attention because it was my calling, born into me.

Maybe I didn't learn it at all. I received and accepted it.

WHEN THE ROCKEFELLER FOUNDATION sent me to Dharamsala in the late '70s to help the Tibetan refugees overcome stage fright for their public rituals, the monks wanted to thank me for my work. They offered to send me to a Tibetan doctor for a medical checkup. I didn't need a check-up; I'd had one before coming to India. *She's a very fine doctor*, they insisted, letting me know that she lectured every other year at Johns Hopkins University. So I accepted their gift and went to see the doctor.

She was a woman in her late fifties. She took my hand and held my pulse. She listened to my pulse for what felt like forty-five minutes. She released my hand and said, "I want to ask you a few questions. You must tell me with total honesty if I am correct or not. That is how I make my diagnosis." I agreed.

"Did your grandfather suffer from a heart attack?" she asked.
"Yes."

"Did your father suffer from manic depression?" she asked.
"Yes."

"Did he take shock treatment?"
"Yes."

"Were you traumatized as a child by loneliness?"
"Yes."

"Have you been in a lot of psychoanalysis?"
"Yes, yes, yes."

I told her how peculiar it was to be examined by a psychic. She said, "Oh, I'm not psychic. First of all, your pulse is as precise as an

MRI. On top of that, I don't need to hold your pulse as long as I did, but I do it to put you in an unusual position, to make you feel awkward. During your awkwardness I look at your face. The art is the art of looking. I must look at your face with no prejudice. I look at you not as a man or woman, neither as an Easterner nor as a Westerner. I look at you as I would look at a tree or at a rock." Everything is written in the face, she explained. Reading it demands training and seeing.

I DREW A PORTRAIT of a friend as a gift for her sixtieth birthday. When I gave it to her, she was appalled. She couldn't look at it, so she stowed it in her attic. The day she sat for me, she later explained, she'd been going through something awful with a family member. Even though her face showed none of this, I had seen the pain behind the face, just as I would see whatever is behind an actor's mask. Had I done the drawing on a different day, it would have been a different drawing, a different face. I spent a long time doing self-portraits and, even though I did them one after another, each one is dramatically different from the others.

THIS WAY OF LOOKING is also how I direct. Each day in rehearsal—or even performance—I ask the actors simply to be where they are, in this day, in this moment. Having learned their lines, they run through the scene a few times a day, day after day, month after month, and year after year. They rarely play it the same way, just as our lives are rarely the same. For example, I leave my studio and walk to the front door. I walk to the kitchen or bedroom and greet Cindy. I may perform this ordinary ritual day after day, and yet it's never the same.

I might say, "Hi, honey, I'm home," but depending on whether my mother just died or I just won the lottery or discovered I'm ill, the tone and, therefore, the meaning will change.

Each time we rehearse a scene in a different way, it creates a new layer of paint over older paint over even older paint. This accumulation can bring out colors we've never seen before. David Hockney writes about painting this way: the different washes that make a watercolor, the successive coats of ink in a print, the strata of observation over time in a portrait—these are the layers that add depth and meaning to a work.

Rehearsing *Uncle Vanya*, for instance, Larry Pine (as Dr. Astrov) would often begin the play's opening scene in a very good mood, because that's the way Larry is, or tries to be. Wally would then enter as Vanya in his usual state of depressive mockery. Larry would pick up his playful spirit. Julianne/Yelena came on next and joined in on everyone's joking, upbeat mood, the party atmosphere. But one day, Larry took the stage in a terrible mood, because of something that had happened that day. Wally came in expecting Larry's good mood, but, hit with a bad one, got even more depressed. Julianne, likewise, expecting everyone to be happy and carefree, wound up in a deeply bad mood. I don't know what was on their minds when they hit this uncharted territory, but I suspect they were wondering how the hell they'd ever get to the end of the play, doing it this way. They did get to the end, though, and in the process discovered an entirely new texture to the play, a layer we'd never known.

WHEN I DRAW MY ERASER is my best friend. The erasures can't be seen by the naked eye, but they are there somewhere, part of the drawing. Likewise, there are thousands of additions and thousands of erasures in each scene, all *in there* somewhere. The text remains the same, but the experience keeps shifting, until, with years of experience under us, the play is all of what we are and all of what we are together. An enormous summation of our days.

One day, of course, the Grim Reaper will erase me.

33

WHEN I'M NOT IN THE ROOM rehearsing with Wally, I dream I'm in a room rehearsing with him. We have had one of the longest collaborations—director/actor and playwright/ actor—in the history of the American theater. Forty-five years and only one fight, when I grew visibly angry over some actors' chaotic schedules. Wally had never seen me like that. It frightened him, and he asked me to stop it. I did. No problem.

Wally's vision is prophetic. He sees the shape of things to come. He anticipates the demons coming down the road. In our first collaboration, Wally's *Our Late Night*, he wrote about the coming of Reaganesque yuppies, who cared only about themselves and their appetites. He wrote it in the 1970s—before there was a

President Reagan, before there were yuppies. Well, yuppies were all around us, but we didn't know it yet. We didn't recognize them for what they were. But Wally saw them.

The Designated Mourner predicted the coming of a Trump-like dictator and frighteningly saw the end of our democracy more than twenty years ago. And *Grasses of a Thousand Colors* is prescient. We are destroying our planet, destroying our food. Wally sees and hears with an awful clarity. We mounted *Grasses* at the Royal Court in London in 2009 and then at the Public Theater in New York (with Theatre for a New Audience) four years later, and even the critics saw how strange and brilliant was his terrifying comic-tragic vision of our poisoned world. Some audiences have trouble with his plays; they are too timid to look. Wake up!

WE'VE WORKED TOGETHER on new plays for years. The same is true of our work on classics: *Uncle Vanya*—four years—*A Master Builder*—fourteen years! And in 2015 we embarked on Ibsen's *Hedda Gabler*—a leap of faith that we have as many years ahead of us as it will take. Wally also translated/adapted *A Master Builder*, as well as portraying the architect, Halvard Solness. By the time we finished rehearsing these classics, however, I felt as though I'd written them, as though they were *mine*. That's how personal the work is. Wally's vision becomes mine. His worldview becomes *ours*.

A MASTER BUILDER is a mysterious play, whose mysteries are usually made murky in translation. Wally's translation eliminated the murk and illuminated the play. Usual theater wisdom sees it as the story of a vengeful young woman, Hilda Wangel, who, when the great architect Solness breaks a promise made to her as a girl, hunts him down and seduces him to his death. Specifically, it is she who convinces the older man to climb the tower of his newest masterpiece, from which he falls to his death.

In this telling, Hilda is a Kali figure, bringing new life through destruction. I saw her as an angel of life and love, of transformation. I thought Ibsen was writing about an artist, stuck and aging, finally able to make his last creative breakthrough, to fulfill his final task, namely the fearless leap into death. A leap of faith with Hilda as an angel of death—just the kind of spirit I would want beside me when my time has come.

Wally's translation illuminated the play and gave it clarity, with the poetry, ambiguity, and strangeness still there, right under the skin. Despite the clarity, Ibsen's structure confused me. The ending confused me, too, including how to stage it: How do we see Solness's fall from the tower? One reason the play took us so many years to rehearse was that we simply could not figure out the ending. And without an ending how can your beginning and middle make sense? Logic, logic, logic.

One day an idea started taking shape: What if Solness is dying from the very beginning? Wally and I were sitting on the couch in my living room, where we usually rehearsed, when he floated the idea. (Or maybe I came up with it. When you work that long and deeply on a play, it's impossible to know who contributed what.) What if the whole production, we wondered, takes place during the final seconds of Solness's life?

As a concept, it reminded me of a favorite childhood book: Charles Dickens's *A Christmas Carol*. I was always fascinated by the story of Ebenezer Scrooge, that awful old miser who is visited on Christmas Eve by the ghosts of Christmas present, past, and yet to come. These visits, as everybody knows, transform him.

He wakes up on Christmas morning, newly loving and generous, ready to plunge into the beauty of life.

So maybe Solness was Scrooge. Saved at the last moment. Illuminated. Awakened. Ecstatic. There is always hope. Love can still appear. It's never too late. I suppose my attraction to this interpretation was rooted in life with my father, in my chronic hope that his depression would end, that he'd wake up to the beauty of his life.

Even later in the process—maybe after another year—Wally took this idea and went further. He invented a staff of nurses who tend to Solness in the final seconds of his life. In the production—and in Jonathan Demme's film of our production—these nurses flowed in and out of the action, dressed in hospital whites and quiet shoes, pulling white curtains around the great man's bed, checking blood pressure, heart monitor, intravenous tube, pulse. Their humming became the sound of medical instruments. Their whispers became sounds heard in the retreating world, their movements the hush of ministering angels. Like Hilda, they are not really there, but are figments of Solness's imagination.

I'm often asked why I rehearse a play so long, longer probably than any director in the world. This is why. Ideas don't come all at once. We expect painters to work on paintings over years, sketch after sketch. We expect novelists to write for years, drafting a book, then throwing out the draft and starting over again and again. Why don't directors work this way, too? Well, I do. With each pass, each improvisation, the work gets deeper. Ideas emerge and the problems you've been wrestling with get solved for real, not with easy solutions or cliché ones, but with answers that go to the heart of the play and the truths the play is exploring.

For almost fourteen years, we had wrestled with how to stage the ending, Solness's fall from the tower. Wally's idea solved the ending in the simplest, most logical way. As Solness ascends the tower, the entire company of nurses simply turns to face the audience. Looking forward and up, they watch an imaginary Master Builder climb an imaginary tower and then plunge to his death. We watch them watch him. We see, in our mind's eyes, what they see.

The strange thing is that when I first read Wally's own plays I don't understand them. I have no idea what they're about. What always attracts me is the complex density of the language, its strange beauty.

WALLY, the "my" of *My Dinner with André*, is actually the center of that movie, even though I do much of the talking. Wally is that rare playwright, like Shakespeare and Molière, who is also a great actor. This is why, in all my productions, I cast him in leading roles.

WHEN I CHOOSE ACTORS I am creating the family I never had. Wally is, of course, the prime example. I have to have a very special affinity with each actor. I have to know them deeply, intuitively. I like intelligent, original, fairly eccentric people. It's like when you fall in love—and I do fall in love with them—you love some still unrecognized, even unfulfilled, part of yourself, a person you would like to be.

BUSBY BERKELEY WAS RIGHT ABOUT CASTING. In his spectacular movie musicals, he knew it wasn't enough to line up a bevy of long-legged, rosy American beauties. Each woman had to fit next to the other, he said, like pearls on a beautiful Japanese necklace. They had to go together, each belonging to the one on either side of her. Each actor has to be absolutely unique, and each has to fit the family.

IN CONVENTIONAL CASTING, you find the best actor, often a star, for a difficult role with a commercial goal, say Ethel Merman in *Gypsy* or Richard Burton and Elizabeth Taylor in *Who's Afraid of Virginia Woolf?*: huge, passionate, terrifying tanks hammering home Edward Albee's play. Unconventional, revelatory casting is another thing. I saw an amazing performance by Elaine May and Mike Nichols in an under-the-radar production of *Virginia Woolf* in Hartford. Instead of screaming at each other and browbeating each other, instead of roaring around the house too drunk to fuck, Mike and Elaine played the roles of George and Martha as soft-spoken academics, intellectual killers who would cut your heart out with lacerating brilliance. They were the big fish in a small academic pond, cruel, deadly, and above all quiet. They, too, were stars, and they were chilling.

EACH GENERATION OF PLAYWRIGHTS creates the actors needed to perform their plays. The forties and fifties, for example, gave birth to Tennessee Williams actors. In part because of the Actors Studio and in part because of the culture of the time, suddenly there were actors like Geraldine Page, Paul Newman, and Marlon Brando, who were themselves Tennessee Williams characters. The way they moved, the rhythms of their speech, their very psyches were born out of the culture that gave rise to these plays. And there was a Tennessee Williams director, too: Elia Kazan.

Williams's plays made these actors and this director necessary. They were made for each other.

And it's the same with Wally. There are great actors who don't live on Wally's planet, and then there are Wally Shawn actors. Wally is, of course, a Wally Shawn actor. Julie Hagerty, as she stunningly proved as Cerise in *Grasses of a Thousand Colors* and again as Aline Solness in Wally's translation/adaptation of *A Master Builder*, lives on Planet Shawn. And as we found, Deborah Eisenberg, the brilliant short story writer and Wally's longtime partner, who had never acted but after years of hard work gave a chilling, devastating performance in *The Designated Mourner*, is from the planet, too.

Not everyone is. The third role in *The Designated Mourner*—Debbie/Judy's father—proved immensely difficult. Howard is an older writer with a dissident past, a fine poet and essayist, a kind of W. S. Merwin figure. It's very, very hard to act brilliance, so Wally's idea was to find a great man/great writer, someone like Harold Pinter. We tried the poet-playwright Derek Walcott, another idea of Wally's. Walcott came to my apartment and read through the play with us. He was excellent. He would play the role, he said, if we rehearsed at his house in St. Lucia and if I gave him a Vuillard painting my father had left me when he died. So Walcott was out. Then I thought of Arthur Miller. Miller, who was perfect for the role—brilliant, sophisticated, condescending; he always seemed to me to belong on Mount Rushmore—actually gave a great public reading with Wally and Debbie at the New York Theatre Workshop for an audience of about forty. Afterward, Miller took me aside. About the play he said, "I didn't understand a goddamn word." About Wally, "But I think the kid's got talent."

34

HAPPINESS NEVER MAKES as good a story as distress, and a life devoted to happiness doesn't, some would argue, make as good an artist as a life devoted to the hard work of art. That was Richard Avedon's argument, and it was the subject of an ongoing argument between us. Until his death in 2004, we would debate whether life should be spent in devotion to work or whether work was just part of making a good life. Dick was clear that work was everything. For me, work and life are inseparable. I can't choose one over the other. My work is my life, and my life is my work.

. . .

I MET DICK when he came to see *Alice* and talked with me afterward. He saw the show many times and then invited us to his studio to shoot the production, where he ultimately held twelve studio sittings with the cast in 1970–71. They comprise, perhaps, the finest collection of photos of a single production in the history of the American theater. They capture the play's momentum, wildness, joy, and acrobatic daring—the great delinquent lunacy of it all: Lewis Carroll blowing Alice up into a parade balloon; the caterpillar smoking his hookah on the backs of four actors who form a mushroom; Humpty Dumpty, an egg smashed on his face, falling from a tower of chairs.

The series became the gorgeous black-and-white book of Dick's photos, the play's script, and text from Doon Arbus's interviews with the Manhattan Project company: *Alice in Wonderland: The Forming of a Company and the Making of a Play*. Months before his death—for my seventieth birthday—Dick printed and framed a wall full of these photos as a gift to me, his final gift, these pictures that introduced me to Dick's brilliant, obsessive intensity and sealed our lifelong friendship.

ALMOST FIFTY YEARS AFTER we met and more than a dozen since he died, I still wrestle with his voice in my head, berating me: I don't commit to my work enough. I'm a dilettante. I should work harder, make more art, keep at it night and day. His voice is ever with me, arguing about this quote from Yeats: "The intellect of man is forced to choose / Perfection of the life, or of the work . . ."

. . .

YEARS AFTER HE DIED, I wrote him a letter. I addressed our long-standing argument. Here it is.

Dear Dick:

This is the letter I had always intended to write but never did. In the months before you died, when you still seemed quite healthy, I had a strong impulse to tell you that I had begun to draw, and that I was loving it. I knew you would hate this—André at seventy, working in an art form with which he had no experience. My retreat to the Cape, too, I knew you wouldn't approve of. Long holidays, you believed, were a waste of precious time. Time should be spent on work.

This disagreement over ways of working and creating was our one deep source of disagreement and friction. This conflict kept us apart at times. Because I loved you, I wanted to explain, but that would take courage, given how fiercely I knew you would disagree. So I put this letter off until it was too late. You died as you'd hoped to—in the saddle.

Let's face it—artists are always working, though they may not seem as if they are. They are like plants growing in winter. You can't see the fruit, but it is taking root below the earth.

You chose work. I have chosen the *life*. The work *and* the life.

At least I have done so in the last 30 years. Doesn't the work on the self inform the *Work*? When we inch closer to ourselves, to who we originally were, who we're meant to be, doesn't that serve the work, doesn't it connect us more deeply to others? Isn't there value in spreading laughter, love, and compassion to the people around us?

I have to say it again with emphasis: *The life and the work are equally important.* You cannot separate one from the other. The work changes the life, and the life changes the work.

You owned that exquisite house in Montauk, one of the loveliest I have seen anywhere, on the cliffs overlooking the ocean. You designed it yourself. But you almost never went there. Did you yearn for another kind of life? Yes, you had friends—almost all driven and workaholic artists—but never a community. You saw each of us alone. In those lovely rooms of yours, over superb dinners, the talk would always be of work, work, and work.

Each time you stopped, you would descend into a depression, believing that you had hit a wall and lost the ability to work, that you would never work again.

So here's what I was afraid to say to you: I'm drawing now, and I love it. I love doing something I don't know how to do, returning to a "beginner's mind." I don't do it for critics or posterity, which was so important to you. Drawing brings out a joyful side of me. Plays tend to be sad affairs, which I try to lighten with laughter. My drawing, though, is all laughter. It returns me to some very early state, a time before loneliness, abandonment, and fear. Happy in that state, I make others happy.

I still hope for your understanding. I still want your blessing. And I miss seeing you at my shows.

Your always friend,

André

35

WHEN *MY DINNER WITH ANDRÉ* first came out, few realized how deeply political it was, because its politics were
expressed in surreptitious ways. From this distance, though, you
can see these major themes: that Americans are falling asleep and
that fascism, in the form of corporate totalitarianism, is coming.
People who are asleep have lost the ability to resist, to say no.

One scene from the movie has reached tens of millions of
people, mostly through YouTube and Facebook. Many of them
probably haven't seen the whole film or ever heard of André
Gregory and Wally Shawn. In the scene André argues that "the
process which creates this boredom we see in the world now may
very well be a self-perpetuating unconscious form of brainwashing

created by a world totalitarian government based on money." André quotes a Swedish physicist who believes that:

> New York is the new model for the new concentration camp, where the camp has been built by the inmates themselves, and the inmates are the guards, and they have this pride in this thing that they've built—they've built their own prison—and so they exist in a state of schizophrenia where they are both guards and prisoners. And as a result they no longer have—having been lobotomized—the capacity to leave the prison they've made or even to see it as a prison.

If we are becoming totalitarian, the movie asks, what do we do? How do we survive morally, ethically, and personally? It's a hard question; each of us has to ask it of ourselves. Nevertheless, we know we have to wake up. We have to act. We have to resist.

"WE CANNOT AFFORD the luxury of despair," the novelist Arundhati Roy warned, as our country and others went to war in Iraq. I agree with her. During the awful Bush years, Cindy and I went to visit our friend and neighbor Howard Zinn. We were devastated by what was happening to this country: immoral wars, torture, "extraordinary rendition" kidnappings. We felt helpless and passive.

I am a disciple of Zinn, who marched with Martin Luther King, Jr., and whose *People's History of the United States* transformed the way we see this country's past. Cindy and I asked him what to do. His answer surprised us. "Of course, you also have to do the usual things," he said. "Protest. Demonstrate. Call your representative. E-mail Washington.

"But most of all," he added, "make your art. Art brings light into the darkness."

I GREW UP IN A EUROPE surrendering to totalitarianism. Europe didn't really fight this totalitarianism; it surrendered to it. I grew up with the Moscow show trials. I grew up with Hitler, my childhood coinciding with his rise and rule. My family—my father especially—was haunted by Stalin. I've become hypersensitive to the possibility of totalitarianism, of fascism.

The situation in the West in 2018 is like that in Weimar, Germany. It scares me. In Weimar, liberal democracy was collapsing. A large mass of frightened, angry, unemployed people rose up to bring Hitler into power. Now we have Brexit, Poland, Hungary, Trump's America. Countries closing borders. Countries turning fascist. Europe either falling apart or paralyzed. America has already been taken over by corporate totalitarianism. Fascism can happen anywhere. I smell it today in America. I hope to God I'm wrong.

LET'S FACE IT: Those of us who are white Americans have been spoiled. What have we had to endure? After all, the Parisians lived through Nazi occupation. Chileans lived through one junta, the Greeks another. The Soviet people have endured unspeakable times. In our country, of course, African Americans and Native Americans continue to fight for freedom and even survival. Marx may have been correct when he said that capitalism would destroy itself. America feels like Weimar, because everything seems to be collapsing at the same time.

· · ·

SHORTLY AFTER THE 2016 ELECTION, I returned to psycho-therapy. The therapist told me I was suffering from post-traumatic stress disorder, that the rise of Trumpism had flooded me with a million forgotten memories. Even in the most blissful time of life, the past can rise up to haunt you.

IN THE EARLY EIGHTIES, when the Solidarity movement began in Poland in opposition to Communist rule under the Soviets, Grotowski was caught between forces. Leaving Poland was, for him, unimaginable. He loved Poland. It was home and the source of his work. Nearly every major group in the country, though, viewed him as an enemy. He had spoken out against the speed with which Solidarity was moving; he felt they were pushing too fast and would set off a Soviet invasion and crackdown. He found himself hated by the protest movement, which also saw the support of his work by the state as suspect. The Catholic Church hated him, too, and saw him as a threat and his work as apostasy. The Communist Party hated him, because he was a mystic. Despised from every side, he worried for his life.

He would appear suddenly in New York, every six months or so, and he and Chiquita and I would talk till dawn. Chiquita, who was as dear a friend to him as I was, had by then made two films about him and his work and videotaped hundreds of hours of his experiments and conference appearances. Jerzy sounded like my father, asking the questions a survivor asks: "What do I do next? Where do I go from here?" Heartbroken but realistic, he made the decision to immigrate to America.

· · ·

JERZY WAITED WITH CHIQUITA at a tacky motel in New Jersey for a meeting with the FBI to work out the specifics of his defection. Meanwhile, he dispatched me to France with a personal letter to be read to each member of his theater company. The Lab members were holding a workshop in a French countryside monastery. The letter explained that he was defecting, and offered them a chance to defect, too, if they wished to do so.

My day at the monastery was truly heartbreaking. I took the members of his company, maybe twenty in all, one at a time into a small room. I gave each of them his letter to read. They could not have been more shocked and appalled. Each actor suddenly faced an unthinkable choice: to return home to Poland or never to return. It was awful for them. The world they had trusted was gone. The man they had trusted was gone. Chaos and panic filled the monastery.

The next day I took them to a lawyer in Paris so they could find out their legal rights, should they stay in France. The lawyer spent the entire day speaking with one after another, until he'd met with everyone. When the day was over, I asked him how much I owed him for all this work. "Nothing," he replied.

"Nothing?"

"Are you not, perhaps, Jewish?" he asked me. "Well then, don't you know that in the Talmud it is written: 'He who saves one life saved the world'?"

WE LIKE TO BELIEVE that Americans care for others. We tell the story that America entered World War II to save the Jews, but in truth we turned them away at our borders if they didn't have money. America has always been a money-grubbing country. We need to admit that ours is an extremely cruel country, too, built on the genocide of Native Americans, built by slavery, by dropping atom bombs. We have to admit our own cruelty, our own evil. If we don't, we will enact and perpetuate it.

36

I DON'T KNOW if any part of us lives on after death, but I like to think the soul does, the part of us that is love and compassion. Everything else in nature continues. When you walk down the street and see a couple who are madly in love, who can't keep their hands off each other, everybody—without thinking—starts moving closer to them. Why is that? It's magnetic. What is that force or energy that magnetizes us? Gurumayi teaches that the soul is the ecstatic state. It's interesting: Some people, when they orgasm, say, "Oh my god! Oh my god!" Maybe there's a connection.

"All souls are beautiful," the guru says. Someone asks her, "Would you invite a criminal, a murderer, to dinner?" Gurumayi answers, "Of course not. That would be silly. But that doesn't mean I can't love his soul."

Leopold and Loeb were two brilliant University of Chicago students who killed fourteen-year-old Bobby Franks as an experiment in committing the "perfect" crime. Leopold became a great teacher in prison. He turned the penitentiary library into a school. You might say his soul opened. I believe it was always there.

I have a fantasy. It happened but of course I wasn't there. I am sitting at a Tuscan café during the early years of the Renaissance. At the next table sits an up-and-coming art star, talking to a friend over a glass of wine: Michelangelo. His work is everywhere these days. Everybody's talking about it. Lots of buzz. "What do I have in mind when I begin to sculpt?" he says to his friend. "Nothing, really. No, I mean it. I simply go to a quarry, choose the largest piece of Carrara marble I can find, and have it sent to Florence.

"No, I swear," he continues in my fantasy. "I have no image in mind. No thought at all about anything. No goal. I just begin to chip away. I take my chisel, and I chip and chip and chip. What finally reveals itself, in spite of me, is the sculpture. I couldn't be more surprised at what I see. Where did it come from? Surely not from me. It came from the stone."

As I contemplate the waning years of a long life, I'm struck by the radical change in my own life through my seventies and eighties. Change for the better. How did this happen in these last years?

You know that game kids play? You hold your arms against your sides and try to raise them as another kid presses them tightly against you, and then lets go. Your arms float up like helium balloons. That's the way it was for me. For years it was tough, and then suddenly it wasn't. I blossomed into myself. I became *me*.

· · ·

IT WOULD TAKE FOREVER to become a lighthouse, illuminated from within, as the great actor Erland Josephson once confessed to me. It wouldn't be easy, and the world with its darkness would try to kill your light. But you keep trying. You keep learning. Maybe you get lucky and meet the love of your life in your sixties. Maybe you take up painting at seventy. Maybe, at eighty-two, you begin rehearsing *Hedda Gabler* with no promise you'll ever finish.

37

I T'S THAT TIME OF YEAR AGAIN—I always dread its
arrival—the time when summer and autumn battle for su-
premacy, a battle that summer inevitably loses. The skies and the
tides grow strange and different. Rougher. Sunset comes by seven,
and so it gets dark early. The crickets sing their farewell song. A
few last stragglers on the Truro beach walk large dogs. Some leaves
have turned red already. The moon rises and sets in another place
in the sky.

The passing of yet another year, more poignant at this time than
in January, when the New Year is usually celebrated. This is our New
Year, the Jewish one: Rosh Hashanah, the beginning of ten Days of
Awe. This year, more than any I remember, I am awed, truly awed, in

the face of enormous change and turmoil, mystery and danger. We will pray for a year that is not awful, a year without an awful war.

Yesterday Cindy and I ate apple slices covered with country honey. We do this every year at Rosh Hashanah to bring in a new year of sweet blessings, something we badly need now. We perform another ritual, *tashlikh*: scattering bread crumbs in the ocean, casting away our sins. This year the waves are almost too high, but we scatter anyway. The waves are huge, remnants of the giant hurricanes down south.

Three consecutive hurricanes have destroyed whole Caribbean islands. There have been two enormous earthquakes in Mexico. And here goes Trump shouting destruction like a ruler gone mad. We live in Old Testament times: wars and pestilence. Worshipping the fatted calf. Mother Nature, going berserk and hurting us so.

This strange summer is over. How to find the sweetness and the blessings in all this darkness? That's the question.

I'm trying to remember something that Tennessee Williams said. I can't call it up exactly. So I climb the stairs to our little guest room, where we keep theater and film books. I search for over an hour. I find it:

The world is violent and mercurial—it will have its way with you. We are saved only by love—love for each other and the love that we pour into the art we feel compelled to share: being a parent; being a writer; being a painter; being a friend. We live in a perpetually burning building, and what we must save from it, all the time, is love.

Yes! Yes!

Back to New York tomorrow, eighty-five summers come and gone. Back to work.

38

J OHN CAGE SAID: "When you start working, everybody is in
    your studio—the past, your friends, enemies, the art world,
and above all, your own ideas—all are there. But as you continue
painting, they start leaving, one by one, and you are left completely alone. Then, if you're lucky, even you leave."

ACKNOWLEDGMENTS

A.G.:

I begin by thanking one of my dearest friends, Mary Anne Schwalbe, for bringing into the world our terrific editor, Will Schwalbe. He has been positive, strong, supportive, warm, clear, logical, self-effacing, and inspired. Throughout the process. His almost invisible hand has been both gentle and firm.

And he pulled a grand rabbit out of his hat. Late in the game, when the book seemed stuck, Will invited a younger editor, Pronoy Sarkar, to join us. Sharp, brilliant, funny, eccentric, jazzy, and original. Pronoy took the book apart and put it together again.

I thank all the brilliant actors who have helped bring my productions to life over these many years, including, of course, Wally Shawn, whose brilliant and prophetic plays have kept me employed for half a century. Wally and these wonderful actors have become my collaborators and chosen family. Thank you all.

Thanks to my friends Eugene Lee, my longtime set director, and Bruce Odland, my composer and sound designer.

Thanks to Louis Malle and Jonathan Demme, who, by reimagining my productions for the screen, allowed them to reach a much larger audience than the stage versions could ever do.

Carol Rizzo, who has been my backup for thirty-one years, has kept me organized and sane.

My dear buddy George Sheanshang not only sealed this deal, but when my knees were a problem, dressed as an elegant chauffeur he wheeled me maniacally through art museums as he has wheeled me through the business of life.

Cindy Kleine, for all her good advice. And laughter. And encouragement. And patience.

Nick Gregory and Marina Gregory, for their continued love and support. They may have taught me more than I taught them.

And so many thanks to my friend the writer Joan Wickersham. Over the years that went into this book, she has advised, guided, and encouraged me when I wanted to throw in the towel.

And finally, my friend Bill Reichblum, who, by believing in this book and bringing Will into it, led me down another stage on the Yellow Brick Road.

And thank you, WHOEVER, for my wonderful life.

T.L.:

This book has been a collaborative effort from the start, not just between André and me, but with many generous friends. I second, word for word, André's big gratitude to Will Schwalbe and Pronoy Sarkar. Will's favorite salutation—"Onward!"—could be heard every step of the way, even as they guided us toward the edge of a cliff.

Special thanks to Sandy Moffett, who introduced me to the work of André and the Manhattan Project when I was his student; to my brother/editor Jim O'Quinn, who suggested I write about André on his seventieth birthday for *American Theatre* magazine, and so got this party started; and to the gracious and singular Wallace Shawn, who spoke to me at length about his life with André, even as I was beginning mine. Much of our work was done while I held the Floyd U. Jones Family Endowed Chair for Drama at the University of Washington School of Drama, and Floyd's generous endowment made my years on this possible. Elizabeth Lee and my pal Josh Beerman kept me from falling into complete organizational chaos. Thanks to the Friday writing group.

Finally, my bottomless gratitude and love to Karen, Guthrie, and Grisha, and the whole Hartman/London family.